YOUTHFUL LONGEVITY

Why Living to 100 Vibrant,
Productive, and Fulfilling
Years is Your Birthright,
and Mandate

ALEX LUBARSKY

authorHOUSE

AuthorHouse™
1663 Liberty Drive
Bloomington, IN 47403
www.authorhouse.com
Phone: 833-262-8899

Published by AuthorHouse 09/13/2024

ISBN: 979-8-8230-3366-4 (sc)
ISBN: 979-8-8230-3365-7 (e)

Library of Congress Control Number: 2024919222

Print information available on the last page.

Dedicated to Ilene Castaldo, Danielle Roberts, Mitchell Kurk, Joshua Rosenthall, Jimmy Kilimitzoglou, and all the brave and honorable doctors who adhere to the Hippocratic Oath and are unwavering in the pursuit of health and happiness for the people they serve.

This books Ikigai, or its purpose for being, is Mila, my first granddaughter and this tangible affirmation that she live to at least 100 vibrant, productive, and fulfilling years.

CONTENTS

CONTENTS

TESTIMONIALS

"Touching. Insightful. Inspirational. This book would make a great movie!" – Mitchell Kurk, MD author of *Prescription for Long Life: Essential Remedies for Longevity.*

"Youthful Longevity is engaging from start to finish. It encompasses Alex's courageous journey back to health as well as those of many other individuals and the non-traditional practitioners who helped them. The book is filled with the wisdom and perspective required to make 100 the New 30 and achieve Youthful Longevity!" – Jeffrey Gladden, MD author of *100 IS THE NEW 30: How Playing the Symphony of Longevity will Enable us to Live Young for a Lifetime.*

"As a physician who practiced general internal medicine for over 30 years and was among the first in the U.S. to form a concierge medical practice, I have always valued an open-minded, "holistic" and personalized approach to patient care. Alex Lubarsky's 'Youthful Longevity' not only aligns perfectly with this philosophy but is deeply enriched by his personal journey. His experiences have fueled a passionate drive for a paradigm shift in healthcare, advocating for a system prioritizing authentic wellness rather than sick care. Alex's work offers a profound understanding of how we can achieve optimal health and longevity and am thankful that he decided to share his wisdom and experience." - Charles F. Glassman, MD, FACP Former owner of The NY Center for Longevity & Wellness; author of *Brain Drain: The Breakthrough that Will Change Your Life*; Host of The CoachMD Podcast.

FORWARD BY JEFFREY GLADDEN, MD

As I read Alex Lubarsky's book, *Youthful Longevity, Why Living to 100, Vibrant, Productive, and Fulfilling, is your Birthright and Mandate*, I was struck by the hero's journey that Alex has been on. Everything from his family escaping the Soviet Union, to his business trials and tribulations in New York, to his ultimate run-in with traditional medicine. Seeing the limitations over and over, it struck me that this is a man who is in relentless pursuit of getting behind all the constructs and all the facades that keep us from stepping into our birthright of living young for a lifetime.

I'm so impressed with Alex's tenacity and determination.

So many people would have given up, so many people acquiesce, so many people adopt the mode of thinking of those around them. I refer to this mode of thinking as binary, where something is either right or wrong and we get attached to a particular answer that precludes other answers. An alternative mode is quantum thinking, where we look at the field of all possibilities, and understand that many things can be true simultaneously. This is analogous to how a quantum computer would sort through all the possibilities to find the best solution. Instead of being attached to an answer, and then looking for evidence to support it, the quantum approach is built on more curiosity and possibility.

As Alex came through his journey, it was those quantum moments when he reached for something different, something that was outside the binary of what he had been taught or told that enabled him to make progress. His contribution to all of us is a beautiful thing to see, because not only does he bear the scars of his journey, but he's also transcended those scars and is genuinely desirous of enabling people to access an alternative life, an alternative medicine, and a new understanding of youthful longevity.

In my world, I think about three different kinds of medicine. There is symptom-driven medicine, which is what I was trained in as an interventional cardiologist. Then there's root cause medicine, which is functional and integrative medicine that I have trained in since.

And then there's longevity medicine.

Longevity medicine is different because it's focused on the actual drivers of aging. Roughly speaking, it's like expertly navigating the current in the Niagara River that gets faster and stronger carrying us downstream towards the Falls.

Alex has taken such a strong step, a bold step, in reiterating that it is our birthright to actually live young for a lifetime. He correctly points out that we are the most fortunate generation of all time to have access to information, technology, insight, and ongoing research that enables us to not only treat the symptoms, and not only get to the root cause of the issue, but to actually address the true drivers of aging. When we approach health and longevity from that perspective, we're able to create the most durable life enhancing solutions possible.

A symptom-driven approach, as Alex points out in his book, is not only fraught with misdiagnosis and mistreatment, but ultimately doesn't solve the problem. Even when it "works", it is only suppressing the symptom, and if the medication or treatment is stopped, the symptom usually recurs.

A functional medicine approach would say, well, let's get to the root cause of the health issue, which is clearly a step forward from symptom-based care. In understanding that the foods we are eating may be causing our leaky gut, which is causing the inflammation, that's ultimately causing your eczema. We have a different approach. Instead of prescribing an immuno-suppressant we can simply help you identify the foods causing the damage, work to heal the gut, address deficiency and toxicity, and allow the skin condition to evaporate like morning dew on a sunny day.

That's the beauty of root cause medicine. But even for people that are treated in this fashion, they're still aging. And it's really the aging process that breaks down our ability to be robust and resilient.

And so, focusing on the Hallmarks of Aging, such as the shortening telomeres, increasing numbers of senescent cells, decreasing mitochondrial function, as well as proteins that don't fold and operate properly. When you start to focus your attention at this level, now you're engaging in longevity medicine.

This is how we make good on the biological aspiration and birthright of living young for a lifetime. And it's such an incredible journey to do this. In my work, our aspiration is that when we're 100 years old, we have a 30-year-old body, and a 300-year-old mind.

I can see that in Alex's work, he's also been growing exponentially in his perspective on the world, and his perspective on himself. And that's what's important, the ability to actually step outside the binary, to step into quantum thinking, to discover new solutions, to understand what the real issues are, not to actually be hemmed in, limited, or brainwashed by what is.

Alex is a true hero in this, in every sense of the word.

And as you read this book, I want you to think about your own hero's journey, and where you are in it and compare it to Alex's. Each one of us has a different hero's journey. But in the end, I wish that you have youthful longevity, that you live young for a lifetime, and that you too will have a 30-year-old body, and a 300-year-old mind and carry that on for the rest of your days.

I think this is our true birthright.

Congratulations to Alex for all his work, all his insight, all his perseverance, and all his generosity in sharing his wisdom, and making available functional medicine to so many.

Jeffrey Gladden, MD is the founder of Gladden Longevity in Irving TX and author of *100 IS THE NEW 30: How Playing the Symphony of Longevity will Enable us to Live Young for a Lifetime.*

INTRODUCTION

Excuse me sir, are you also a doctor? Asked an elderly man after hearing me speak with a physician friend of mine in the waiting room of his office.

I am, to the great disappointment of my mother, not a doctor of any kind. I answered with a smile.

And it's true.

I didn't go to medical school; I am not board certified in one of the many specialties. I don't wear a white coat, or a stethoscope around my neck. Nor am I licensed by any state, province, or nation to practice anything that would allow me to place my hands on your body … legally.

And although, I did not spend years studying how to become a medical sommelier, dramatically pairing chronic conditions with chemical concoctions. I have become something of a passionate advocate on behalf of the human body's ability to restore optimal function, while bringing a semblance of sanity to our system of healthcare delivery. Primarily by scraping off the layers of bureaucracy, built up like paint on a pre-war windowsill, and restoring that sacred relationship between the most brilliant and courageous doctors, with the more open minded among us within the public.

Over the years I've met some of the most remarkable people who have dedicated their lives to taking care of those who are sick or injured. They became nurses and doctors who put themselves through years of schooling at tremendous expense, both in time and money. They went through rigorous training and worked many shifts in a row during residency. Walking the polished floors of large hospitals under the constant glare of florescent lights, usually exhausted and hungry and stressed. Tending to patients dealing with all kinds of health problems, and attitudes.

I witnessed this caring firsthand when my seven-year-old son was hit by a car and rushed to the emergency room. I saw it when my cousin was shot by criminals robbing his jewelry store, and his life saved by those incredible people in the operating room. And once more when my daughter was born, I saw them work tirelessly to take care of my wife and bring this child safely into this world. So, if you hear an edge to my voice, it is not aimed at these beautiful professionals by any stretch of the imagination. My frustration is with this third-party controlled, almost five trillion-dollar tsunami of indefinite management of chronic disease (IMCD) industrial complex, and the perverse incentives that propel it towards our shining city on the hill.

My tone and tenor, as I deliver this message, is one I would take with a close friend. The many remarkable people I've known for decades and some for over forty years. With whom I can be honest. With whom I can be myself. This, I believe, allows for true communication where everything that is said is meant and everything that is meant is said. I hope you will grant me permission to be that upfront and honest with you. I may be wrong, and we can talk about that, but you won't find me hesitant or unctuous, saying what I think you may like to hear so that perhaps I can sell more books, or gain your favor. For that you will either love me and we can be friends, or you will be aghast, and we won't be. Either way, we'll know through this journey where we both stand, and if our missions align.

After my own very unpleasant, life-altering diagnosis some 20 years ago I became determined to understand why modern medicine refuses to cross the line from acute, emergency, triage care to a more proactive, preventative, cause-focused approach. One that looks to resolve a chronic symptom before it explodes into a health catastrophe.

Certainly, we've all heard that an ounce of prevention is better than a pound of cure, but somehow, this almost five trillion-dollar bureaucracy did not get the memo. And is simply providing a ton of over-the-top disease management in the form of surgery, medication, and hospitalization.

Additionally, is it possible for us, mere layman to create the proper circumstances, and empowering context, for a system of care that helps our body find homeostasis. So that it can function at the peak level of health expression, and for an extraordinarily long time, as intended and designed.

To find some answers to the resolution of my own 'incurable' health challenges, I first started reading books by some of the top functional medicine doctors in the country. Remarkable physicians and out of -the box thinkers like Bernie Siegel, Michael Roizen, Gary Null, Mark Hyman, Leigh Erin Connealy, Joel Fuhrman, Steven Gundry, Jeffrey Life, Richard Linchitz, Mitchell Kurk and hundreds of other doctors, and scientists at the forefront of this wellness revolution. As well as celebrity advocates like Suzanne Somers, Carol Alt, Fran Drescher, and Jack LaLanne to name a few. Brilliant and rebellious people who were not going to stand for a system of so-called 'health' care that could not, or would not, bring permanent relief to their own chronic health challenges, nor to the people in their life, or under their care.

Then I started traveling the country, attending many of the professional conferences where I could hear these healers and rebels, with prestigious medical pedigrees, generously share their wisdom. They would explain the science and philosophy behind an entirely revolutionary approach to creating the structures for peak performance function. An inspiring paradigm, one in direct contrast, to the antiquated status quo bureaucracy of indefinite management of chronic disease (IMCD) industrial complex. This light in the darkness, this hope in the depth of despair and medical tyranny, is now better known as functional medicine. As in the opposite of this current model of dysfunctional juggernaut, a multilayered bureaucracy that we've accepted as the norm, and embraced as the only viable option.

Once I had a basic understanding of the human body's miraculous ability, indeed yearning, for self-repair and homeostasis, as well as its simple demands to restore optimal function, I began organizing conferences of my own. We would host as many as 80 lectures at our events by some of the most renowned doctors, healers, bestselling authors and celebrity advocates from around the world. There would be around 150 exhibiting companies and a few thousand people would attend the two-day biannual conference. We held one event in Midtown Manhattan in the spring and the other on Long Island in the fall. For over 15 years I would help those brilliant doctors and healers write articles that went into our publication. I had videographers record their presentations that I would help edit, and I interviewed many of them on our radio program. I read and studied hundreds of their books that still strain the shelves and overflow storage boxes throughout my office and home. We also had more candid conversations one-on-one in my car, and over dinner, when I sometimes picked them up from the airport and drove them to the event venue.

So, although I am definitely not a state licensed doctor of any kind, I am someone who used all this information, science, and technology to permanently resolve numerous 'incurable' conditions, that would have by now permanently crippled me, bankrupted my family, and made life unbearable. Or worse. Had I first gone for a medical degree however, as my father insisted, I would most likely never have been open to exploring anything outside of the established dogma, of a pill for every ill, corporate medicine paradigm. Primarily because you can't change a bad system with people indoctrinated by it and enriched through it. If change is possible, it can only be achieved with the good, honorable, and courageous people the system tried to destroy.

Over the years I've tried hundreds of therapies, supplements, nutritional protocols, exercise regimens, detoxification programs, and exotic medical approaches on the forefront of science and technology. And at times on the very edge of its farthest fringes. Trying to find a modality, or a combination of modalities that would offer a permanent resolution to my detrimental diagnosis.

In this book, along with my team of remarkable physicians, (Danielle Roberts, DO [Chapter 9], Joshua Rosenthal, MD [Chapter 10], and Jimmy Kilimitzoglou, DDS [Chapter 11] as well as the Intro by Jeffrey Gladden,

MD) I'll do my best to introduce you to a revolutionary approach to a more proactive and personalized system of care we call Science of Human Optimization. A multifaceted philosophy that helped thousands of people find their way to better health, and at times permanently resolve the underlying cause of their 'incurable' health challenges. If this current industrialized medicine complex gives that kind of healing any credence at all, it typically puts it in the dubious file of spontaneous remission, or misdiagnosis. So, either the symptom resolved miraculously on its own, or it was never there in the first place, and you just imagined it.

We'll discuss some of the inherent problems with our almost five trillion-dollar hodgepodge of indefinite management of chronic disease (IMCD) industrial complex, amusingly and speciously referred to as the best *health* care system in the world. One that's controlled by politics, lobbyists, unions, looming insolvency, and is fraught with perverse incentives and moral hazards. We will also shatter some of the misconceptions, propaganda, and outright lies that have brought us to this sad, indeed lugubrious state of ill health, obesity glut, daily suffering, and early demise.

Conditions that were not long ago an aberration among mankind confined to ticketed viewing, like the bearded lady or the fat man, are today the societal norm. Indeed, body-positivity and fat shaming, are some of the recent philosophical anomalies that entered the English lexicon. Normalizing and celebrating a deadly trend. Finding a thin, healthy, and vibrant adult who is not dependent on a symptom-suppressing chemical cocktail, and some kind of therapy for daily function, is the outlier.

One thing you can be sure of, right or wrong, I am not beholden to any organization. I am not controlled and manipulated with the threat of losing my medical license by some woke association, pompous bureaucrat, or evil conglomerate. I have no interest in money for money's sake. And respectfully, I could not care less of what anyone thinks about me, my position, or ideas.

I know for a fact that instead of focusing on suppressing a particular symptom, if we would only look to optimize the body by making sure it has all the necessary nutrients, heal and optimize the system of digestion, adjust our nutrition and lifestyle, and remove toxicity such as heavy metals and parasites, this organic miracle that you are kind enough to wash and dress each morning, will find its way back to vitality, optimal function, and youthful longevity. Over the last 20 years I've experienced this personally numerous times and watched so many others find what can only be called spontaneous remission miracles, as they regain their health, and create their best life.

Now all we need to do is build the proper context. A system of human optimization if you will. One that allows for an ongoing, life-long relationship between those with the fiduciary responsibility to keep us living in abundance, with that life giving energy that powers this experience for the duration of our extraordinary long, prosperous, and meaningful lives. While at the same time helping us circumvent the many chronic illnesses we have come to accept as inevitable and incurable. You are already betting a substantial fortune to insure against the financial catastrophe that comes along with a devastating health problem. I want to invite you to consider hedging your bet. In the chance that through the art and science of human optimization you can avoid the devastating health problem in the first place.

And here I ask you, what investment is more valuable, or endeavor more worthwhile, than connecting the y-axis of your healthspan (how well you live) with the x-axis of your lifespan (how long you live)? What's more important than keeping ourselves and those we love functioning optimally for as long as possible?

Nothing. Absolutely nothing. Hua!

By the way, in Latin, "doctor" means teacher. So, if you will allow me, in these next pages, I'll be your doctor, friend, preacher, and entertainer.

Mom will be so proud.

Chapter One

HOPE

If you're still alive, anything can be cured and
if you don't believe that, nothing can.

By the time the doctor walked into the small and chilly exam room I had
waited for over a month to see him. My journey began some twenty years
ago, with a small patch of dry skin just above my right ear. I was in my
mid-thirties and had not visited a doctor since that wintery morning in a
Moscow hospital, many Octobers ago, when I was born.

At first, I just put butter on it, and every kind of cream and lotion I could
find in my wife's vanity, to try and ease the inflamed, dry, and flaky skin.
But as time went on the lesions began to spread. Soon after I found another
spot near the ankle of my left leg. And within a few years, red patches
covered some 60% of my body, including both sides of my head. One of
the dermatologists I went to said that in all his 25 years of practicing he
never saw a case as severe as mine.

What can I say, I'm an overachiever.

That was bad, but even worse, my joints began to hurt. My hips, wrists,
fingers. The hips were so bad in fact that I could hardly get myself out of
a seated position without assistance, and when I walked, I moved like a
90-year-old man after a heavy leg day.

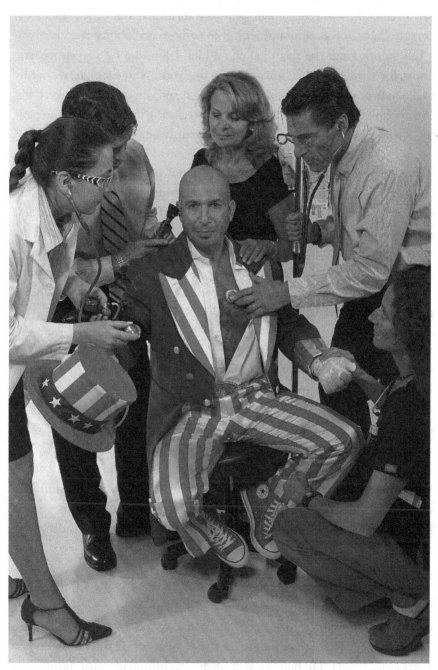

Making America Healthy Again

So, after a few months of dealing with that small patch above my right ear, I reluctantly dug up our health insurance card and called up a local dermatologist for an appointment. The earliest availability they had was a full month from the day I called. Which I found a bit surprising, you know, for 'the best health care system in the world'. Interestingly, we hardly make such braggadocio claims about our gas stations or supermarkets, but I've never had trouble getting filled up, or accessing the abundant vegetable section of a local grocery store, instantaneously and affordably.

That morning I showed up about 15 minutes early and promptly sat in the waiting room for over an hour flipping through the many magazines stacked on the glass coffee table in front. Mercifully one of the humorless and heavyset front desk personnel waved me over and escorted me to the meat locker they called an exam room. Where I sat impatiently, next to a full sized, expressionless skeleton in the corner, along with all the posters of frightened people exhibiting advanced cases of my insipient condition, plastered on the walls.

I waited there for 20 or so minutes before the good doctor finally walked in. He was a nice enough man, obviously very busy and after a quick introduction, I pointed to the side of my head, to answer his question of what brought me in to see him. He quickly offered a diagnosis. A debilitating, life-altering and incurable condition usually referred to as the 'heartbreak of psoriasis'. Perhaps it's called that, because while it does not kill you immediately, after stealing your ability to do so many of the things that make life worth living, it kind of makes you wish it would. The doctor wrote out his prescription, gave me a sample steroid cream, wished me luck, and three minutes later he was out the door, quickly heading over to the next patient.

'Psoriatic arthritis' was the actual diagnosis, that I've come to learn some years later, and from a different source. But there was no way this doctor could have known that in the brief moments we spent together, even if he was interested. He did not know my family history. He did not know my nutritional habits. He had no idea of my environment, toxic burden, or genetics. He did not know how I process stress, the health of my digestive biome, how well I sleep, how much sugar I consume, or if my body had all the minerals and vitamins it needed for optimal function.

The only thing he knew was that my flaky skin, labeled psoriasis, needed a steroid cream, so we can temporarily suppress the only evidence of an underlying health problem. In other words, I had a fire in my belly, and he was swatting at the smoke. So, this is the modern version of the original, white tent on the battlefield, triage medicine incarnate. Where the system collects as much money as it can in the form of premiums, employer contributions and taxation. Then doles out just enough time to band-aid and numb the well-established condition, sending you back to the grind as quickly and inexpensively as possible.

Additionally, as all this money accumulates in the insurance companies' coffers, presumably to cover emergency health care expenses of their clients, when the government steps in with their own exotic ideas of how to spend it. Driven by the winds of politics du Jour they mandate your insurance company to cover things like sex reassignment surgeries, late term abortions, hair transplants, pre-existing conditions, limitless covid 19 testing, keeping "children" on your insurance plan until they are 26 years old, and of course the unfettered access to all the emergency rooms in the United States, both for people who are here legally and otherwise. Then, when you or your family need access to actual care, the expense grows exponentially, while the value, quality, and access fall precipitously.

Maybe you had the misfortune of experiencing this firsthand when making a trip to the local emergency room. Sitting there like a refuge, in an overcrowded holding facility for hours on end, till they sent over some exhausted, entry level nurse to pacify you.

Many years ago, my wife could not sleep because she had a high fever and sore throat. At first, she just tried to suffer through it, but it was bad enough that we decided to drive to the local emergency room for the first time in our lives. When we got there the waiting room was packed and looked like they were in the middle of some national emergency that created an influx of a motley crew of humanity injured during some sort of catastrophe. Once we finally signed in, they asked us to wait till we were called. Six hours later, we were finally escorted to an exam room where a nurse took her vitals. When the doctor finally appeared, he looked more tired and pained than we were. He spoke with us for a few minutes, glanced at the chart, and prescribed that she go home, rest, and eat some ice cream to cool the inflammation.

Every benefit that the government negotiates on your behalf accomplishes two things, first it shamelessly purchases your vote with your own money, and second it rases either the cost to provide the services you need or limits your access to them.

KILLER HEALTHCARE

Perhaps you are one of the 70% of the US population taking a prescription medication to manage some kind of symptom of some underlying health problem. Maybe you were diagnosed with diabetes, heart disease, cancer, insomnia, fibromyalgia, arthritis, eczema, depression, or (   ). In fact, according to the ICD 10, the US clinical modification lists some 70,000 diagnostic codes, cataloging every kind of possible symptom of a rapidly disintegrating national health reserve and lifespan potential.

Of course, the almost five trillion-dollar indefinite management of chronic disease (IMCD) industrial complex spends some 60 billion dollars per year for a brilliant marketing campaign convincing you that it is your human frailty, indolence, genetics, and inability to diet and exercise regularly that is ultimately at the root of this chronic disease tsunami, driven by an obesity epidemic of idiopathic origins.

But let us fire up the Flux Capacitor and take a trip back to 1955, when the United States spent just 27 billion dollars per year on health care. No one needed to talk to us about the importance of diet and exercise and yet, somehow, we were relatively thin and mostly healthy as a nation. Just look at some of the vintage photos from that era, the people looked good and were thin, even though they were chain smoking, binge drinking, meat grilling, free loving, and experimenting with illicit substances, while consuming lots of real butter and bacon and washing it down with a Budweiser. They also had no gyms, jogging paths, palates studios, health influencers, marathons, or yoga gurus to speak of.

Why is that? "Think McFly, Think!!"

So, if we are going to diagnose our system of healthcare and seek to grasp the underlying cause of its debilitating malfunction, we should look for it somewhere between then and now. We were spending 27 billion dollars per year then and over 148 times that today, and we are quickly headed for 60% obesity, and 100% dependence on a system of indefinite management of chronic disease that speciously promises to relieve suffering, cure disease, and help the sick.

Where did we go wrong?

Why does the context of our system of care, as well as the politics that have been driving it, come up so short when it comes to our healthspan potential and lifespan outcomes? Does it have anything to do with the tyranny of the masses subjugating the autonomy of the individual, by pushing concepts that have been proven unworkable at best, and diabolically murderous at worst?

When the four-year old Noah, son of Joshua McAdams and Taylor Bland-Ball was diagnosed with acute lymphoblastic leukemia, his parents opted to treat him with cannabis, oxygen therapy, herbs and alkaline water rather than chemotherapy. After a multi-state hunt, they were found in Kentucky and lost custody of their son for "refusing to follow up with lifesaving medical care" according to police. This young family that was originally from Tampa Bay Florida, were of course doing what they thought best for their child. But now that the government, as the enforcement arm of a system of healthcare that is also controlled by the same government, is able to force parents to provide state mandated medical care, I imagine that losing your child because you refuse experimental vaccines, public education, or sex reassignment mutilation, is not far behind.

There is a lot of debate in today's political landscape on the merits, of the government controlling the means of production, as a viable and caring system of economics for the future of the United States. Unimaginable just a few short years ago. Perhaps for the first time in the history of this nation, or at least in the over 45 years that I've lived here, that prominent politicians are running for the highest office in the land as full out socialists. Supported by a groundswell of angry, chronically high, spoiled rotten, overweight, poorly dressed, pierced, tattooed, and miseducated teenagers with permission to cast a vote, and not a lucid clue in that smoke and propaganda filled cranium.

But this did not happen overnight. The impetus of this destructive philosophy began a long time ago and grew as a weed in fertilized soil. Only in a prosperous and tolerant system of free market capitalism can this something-for-nothing philosophy flourish like no other place on earth. It's very easy to be a communist or socialist in a capitalistic country, but if you try it the other way around, you will quickly find a dungeon, or a bullet.

A bullet for which your family will be billed.

Sure, there was the USSR that first embraced the flawed hallucinations of Marx and Engels in 1917 permitting Lenin and Stalin to bring the iron curtain down around its impoverished, enslaved, and miserable shores. Then there's China, North Korea, Cuba, Viet Nam, and Venezuela more recently to name but a few examples of societies that embraced this flawed philosophy, like an idiot a cactus. Both the impetus and outcome were always the same, first they rejoiced as they fired their AK 47's into the sky. Then they starved, lived in poverty, cold, and fear, sold out their neighbors, ate their pets, and brutally murdered millions of their own citizens in the name of fairness, equity, and inclusion.

Here in the United States, however, the most productive and successful country in the history of mankind. Not to mention, one of the most generous and patient did this brutal and demonic concept take root and shoot through the clouds as the bean stalk, from Jack and the Beanstalk fame. Sending its evil roots deep into the affluence born out of generations of hard work, dedication, creativity, frugality, investment, blood, toil, tears and sweat, in the pursuit of excellence.

And as in that famed fairytale, it is only a matter of time till we awaken the hungry giants of depravity and maleficence who are going to want to grind our bones into flour to make their bread. Because unfortunately, this flawed eutopia offers little else at the free-lunch banquet, one that it sells with so much hype and sizzle.

AMERICAN LIBERAL

Of course, if you are like most people in this nation, and around the world, you don't want to see anyone going without food or proper medical care. I imagine that one would need to be a sociopath of some kind to watch others suffer and feel nothing … do nothing. How can anyone see a child in pain or her mother hungry and not want the suffering to end. Where, other than New York City perhaps, can you find people callous enough to step over the sad humanity that made the cold sidewalk their bed, and the lonely streets their home.

But please make no mistake, we care, and having lived in New York for most of my adult life, I've seen this caring firsthand, as regular people go out of their way to try and help those who are less fortunate or have hit a troubled patch in their life. Sadly, the problem has become so overwhelming and systemic that no one person can make much of a difference. It seems like the wealthier we become as a nation the less we are able to help those who need it most. And some, who are more practical in their observation, may say that we are complicit in the escalation of this new class of glassy-eyed nomad in the worn sleeping bag, camped out on the streets of major US cities.

Funny thing about the war on poverty, the war on cancer, and the war on drugs, is that the more this army of bureaucrats with pocket protectors, and Che Guevara t-shirts attempt to interfere with basic economics, the worse things become.

9

Here's what Ronald Regan had to say on the topic:

"Anytime you and I question the schemes of the do-gooders, we're denounced as being against their humanitarian goals. They say we're always "against" things-we're never "for" anything. Well, the trouble with our liberal friends is not that they're ignorant; it's just that they know so much that isn't so."

And as much as I love this quote and the man who coined it, I'd like to offer a small caveat. The word 'liberal' with its original meaning stemming from Latin, 'liberalis' described a free person, someone unrestricted, and unimpeded. In his classic book *Capitalism and Freedom*, Milton Freedman, a renowned economist and Nobel Prize recipient, goes into detail about the origins of this sobriquet and the distinction in meaning. This was how the founding fathers of this great nation saw themselves, and until recent history, so did those of us who treasure our independence to live life on our terms, and ability to speak our mind without threat of a public flogging, or a stint in a gulag.

Those who yearn for the safety and security of a government job, on the other hand, the little tyrants and dictators filled with fear and trepidation, gifted the power of the state to forcibly deprive people of their money, reputation, freedom, and property, so that they can mint more dependents born of their munificent malevolence. People who advocate wealth transfer in the form of socialized medicine, government schools, or the nationalization of industry cannot be called liberal. They are the miniature and comical embodiment of the worst despot of the twentieth century.

The mirror image of the worst of human nature and its potential for evil.

When I shared my somewhat untampered view of politicians, and people who are attracted to politics with my thirty-year-old son, he said "Dad, I think I want to go into politics!" Ok, so let me make this clear, in my mind, politics should be the way you serve your country. Once you become successful in the real world, build a business, raise a family, make something of yourself, then as a way to give back to this great nation you offer your time and your money to support and protect the system that permitted your prosperity and happiness. It is not what you want to do, it is your duty, so you do it. This way you can do your part to protect this fragile idea that is the United States of America and safely hand it down to future generations. That is the opposite of the likes of Chuck Schumer and his ilk, who after graduating from an elite university as a lawyer, got a job in politics and then "never done an honest day's work in his life" sort of speak.

Perhaps I can illustrate what I mean better with a scene from the movie Gladiator. When Marcus Arelius the Roman Emperor, invites Maximus, his accomplished and beloved general, to discuss what he most desires from life. Once the great warrior describes his home with pink stones that warm with the sun, and a kitchen garden that smells of herbs in the day, and jasmine in the evening. And how more than anything he wants to go to be with his wife and child once the military campaign is over. After listening carefully, the king invites Maximus to succeed him as the protector of Rome and its new emperor. "With all my heart, no." was the instantiations reply. "Can't you see Maximus, that is why it must be you." Marcus Arelius asserted. Unfortunately, as this mostly fictional story goes, his son Commodus, who was a spoiled, selfish, egotistical, weak, and cruel man, smothers his elderly father before he could make the announcement, and takes the throne by subterfuge.

So maybe it's not the lack of resources or desire but our attitude and belief system that's contributing to these modern social problems. This may explain why a person born in poverty, with no access to education and enduring the worst kind of living conditions, one day awakens to build a successful business and becomes wealthy, happy, and successful. As soon as they do, however, they make a silent vow that their children will never have to go through the same forging between hammer and anvil they endured and experience the hardship that fostered their own ability to succeed against all odds in the first place. Subsequently pampering their offspring in such a way as to make them devoid of any ambition, self-control, or independence.

Certainly not in all cases but we have seen it often enough for it to be the rule more than an exception. Of course, it's easier to spend your life sleeping-in late, drinking Frappuccino's, wearing branded clothing, and enjoying the world's many pleasures, rather than working hard and practicing delayed gratification. But that's like trying to subsist on cake. Chocolate mousse is my favorite, but if I have it once per year, on or around my birthday I can really get some pleasure as I place a generous forkful of that heavenly creation in my mouth, sending my tastebuds and neurons spinning. Should I have had parents who fed it to me at every meal however, I would quickly lose any appreciation for sweets, but worse, what was once heaven, quickly becomes its opposite.

RODENT EUTOPIA

To illustrate this point, a Biologist by the name of John Calhoun conducted a social experiment in 1968 at the National Institute of Mental Health in Maryland. You've probably heard about this, his twenty fifth attempt, at designing a rodent eutopia. The creation of the perfect environment for a group of mice, to see how they behave over a period of time in a manmade wonderland of no work and all play that would have impressed Walt Disney and turned Mickey commie.

He built an elaborate space, with private rooms, plenty of food and water, and a comfortable living area that was safe from any potential predators or worries. So, this group of eight albino mice won the proverbial Powerball jackpot and were provided with everything their little hearts desired for cradle to grave comfort, happiness, health, and longevity.

Within 18 months the population was thriving as it grew to some 2200 offspring over six or so generations. But then something went terribly wrong. There was lots of infighting for no particular reason, the males lost interest in sex, some became obsessed with their looks and groomed themselves for most of the day. Mothers abandoned their pups and eventually the entire population collapsed, and within five years Calhoun's experiment #25 was dead, literally, and figuratively.

Ok, perhaps it's a stretch to correlate the social behavior of mice and men, but at least we can get a glimpse of our own modern-day society, as up becomes down, black turns to white, and water to sand. While the powers that be attempt to remake human nature and make things as comfortable as possible for us in this over the top, smothering with leisure, cradle to grave experiment, #26.

The political class wants to sell us on free healthcare, rent control, food stamps, universal basic income, student loan forgiveness, and the idea that somehow, we can structure economics so that we never have to work. As we enjoy life to the fullest, pursue our passions, hobbies, and pleasures, and get our chicks for free. Of course, the good life, one free of responsibility and worry, is an easy sale, compared to the work hard, be industrious, and save your pennies, so that you can one day enjoy the fruits of your labor. And perhaps more importantly, become the kind of person through that struggle and effort that you would be proud to see in a mirror, and introduce to others.

UNAFORDABLE CARE

When Medicare and Medicaid were signed into law by Lyndon B. Johnson in 1965, it was this paternalistic mindset of a wealthy society allocating resources to provide unobstructed access to health care for the most vulnerable of our population. The elderly and the indigent could now see a doctor, while the government, or perhaps more accurately, the taxpayer, or even more accurately, you and me, cover the bill. A bill that no one bothered to look at prior or question till it came due. The cost expectations were modest during the rhapsodized and unctuous sales process. But as with any of these kinds of third-party payer programs, it quickly got out of hand. Today it is a political third rail; and at a rapidly approaching five trillion dollars per year, it may as well be made from solid gold.

Who in their right mind would challenge this well entrenched entitlement program and try to curtail its unsustainable trajectory. No matter how dangerously unsustainable it may be. So, each subsequent generation of transient politician, be they Democrat or Republican, hangs other additions on it, like ornaments on a giant evergreen during the holidays. Drug benefits, lab tests, cat scans, hospice care, nursing homes, and red

13

bow-tied wheelchair scooters, in every color of the rainbow, for anyone who may want one.

How fitting for those who still believe in Santa.

To solve this unprecedented intrusion into the free market by the government, the government imposed the nationalization of this entire industry with the very unaffordable, unsustainable, and oxymoronic Affordable Care Act (ACA), signed into law in the dead of night March 23, 2010, by he who shall not be named. The crowning star of this bureaucracy, one the size and girth of a Ford F-150, carefully balanced on the very top of this proverbial Christmas tree.

START OF THE END

It was back in 1948 that Harry S. Truman, the thirty third President of the United States, dropped the figurative bomb on the United States when he first began pushing for a national system of government-controlled healthcare. Coming off Franklyn D. Roosevelt's successful implementation of The New Deal, which included the Social Security Act, taking the biggest leap in paternalism, and one could say socialism, in US history up until that time.

Here's what he said.

"The greatest gap in our social security structure is the lack of adequate provision for the Nation's health…This great Nation cannot afford to allow its citizens to suffer needlessly from the lack of proper medical care."

Well, perhaps that was true then, but now as it grows geometrically and heads full speed to five trillion dollars per year, we literally cannot afford this medical bureaucracy either. We cannot afford the tsunami of lifestyle diseases it fostered, the abdication of personal responsibility it encouraged, the tyrannical power it wields, and we cannot afford it to go on for another minute, less it implodes and takes this great Nation down with it.

With hindsight being what it is, perhaps we can understand how the Twentieth Century's infatuation with socialism, and the glory of the communists of the Soviet Union in their valiant fight against fascism by our side, influenced the thinking of our political leaders. But make no mistake, Stalin was a worse despot than Hitler, and operating under a system that was no less brutal, evil, or deadly. In fact, I would argue much more so. Strangely, the one thing those two psychopaths had in common was their enthusiastic support of free (government controlled) medical care for their people. Those same people that they had no compunctions imprisoning, torturing, and executing on a whim, and en masse.

In 1949, in his book *Compulsory Medical Care and the Welfare State*, Melchior Palyi, a distinguished, internationally recognized economist, and American citizen of Hungarian decent, tried to warn the world of the inherent dangers of this bankrupt ideology. Saying:

"In Democracies the Welfare State is the beginning and the Police State the end. The two merge sooner or later, in all experiences, and for obvious reasons. All modern dictators have at least one thing in common. They all believe in Social Security, especially in coercing people into governmentalized medicine."

And that's how we got to where we are today. It took many decades and the continued push by those political leaders, who are not happy with the United States being a capitalist country founded on the principles of independence and self-actualization. Indeed liberalism. So, they set out to bring back the old-world oligarchy, where a few control the many, and one that our founders fought to extricate themselves from, back to our shores. Using revered educational institutions, trusted government agencies, and that pillar of democracy the free press, to sell this democratic version of a demonic vision to the youth and public of our nation, as a new social experiment, one with a long and bloody history, and predictable outcome.

The only way they can keep these programs afloat today, as they inevitably run out of other people's money, is by printing unprecedented trillions of funny money. Flooding the economy with this counterfeit, valueless

15

currency, sending inflation soaring, as the savings of the population dilutes, and prices on basic commodities skyrocket.

AIN'T NO FREE LUNCH

Of course, I did not know any of this surreptitious backstory as I innocently took my health insurance card over to the doctor's office. Thinking that our goals are aligned, with me wanting the permanent resolution of my incipient chronic illness, and this well-established, and well-intentioned medical professional using his education and experience to help me get there. Maybe you were under the same innocent, and somewhat credulous impression. Unfortunately, that is not how our system of healthcare works. I hate to be the bearer of bad news, but this is not the business model, as it were.

As I took my health problem from one doctor to the next, it felt like I was talking to the same person, no matter where I went or what they looked like. Whether I consulted with two or twenty different physicians, with framed diplomas and crystal awards from respectable institutions adorning the walls and shelves of their modern offices, technically I saw the same doctor many times over. The same education, philosophy, mindset, and business model. They all recommended steroid creams, pain medication, biologics, and immuno-suppressing drugs with a rarely fatal infection black box warning, while confidently asserting that psoriatic arthritis has no known cure.

And sure, maybe I can enjoy some clear skin for a couple of years by shutting off my immune system following their advice. But then how embarrassing would it be, when my friends visit me in hospice, asking themselves: "what happened? He was always so healthy, ate so well, and took such good care of himself."

The politicians selling us on this socialized medicine approach never mention that once you buy into it, it will not be able to help you in any meaningful way when you inevitably end up needing it most. It's like getting a free library card to a building with no books. And if we think about it even for a moment it becomes one of those no brainers. As intelligent people who have families, jobs, businesses, homes, cars, and have been dealing with the reality of this world for decades, we clearly understand that we always get what we pay for.

And that, *there ain't no free lunch.*

If someone tries to sell us something that seems too good to be true, we inherently know that there's a catch, and being tarred and feathered is likely, and most probably, not far behind. So how can we for a moment imagine that a self-serving, mendacious, egomaniac who holds political office for decades on end, and spends their entire existence insulated from life's realities while feathering their own nest with silver and gold, is going to manipulate the economy and medical system with magic and sorcery so as to give us valuable services of highly trained professionals free of cost. Regardless of its inherent value or limited supply, simply because it's in our best interest, and because they care so very much.

That's like a pickpocket offering to give you unlimited access to the exclusive wine list of the finer restaurants in town free of charge, if you would just let him hold your wallet.

That of course is ridiculous. And so is this.

~

FINAL THOUGHT

"Hope is the companion of power, and mother of success; for who so hopes strongly has within him the gift of miracles." — Samuel Smiles

Chapter 2

I AM WHO I AM

My word is not a sail driven by the winds of
circumstance; it is the stone on which they break.

The green faded paint on the walls of this small, foul-smelling office in the basement of our school was pealing in numerous places. The man about to provide medical assistance was a giant. Since I was only about 6 years old, most adults were. I was sitting in a well-worn dental chair as he proceeded to start the loud and frightening machinery, he will be using to drill one of my baby teeth. This was over a decade after Soviet Russia put the first man into space. They were using all their resources to impress and frighten the world and had few left over to provide basic services to their population.

Even the children.

There was no Novocain, the local anesthetic discovered and brought to market by Alfred Einhorn in 1905, and quickly made available throughout the civilized world. So as the spinning drill connected with my molar, the only way I could express my displeasure, was to upchuck the thin and bland borsht from lunch all over the good doctors' shoes and the well-trafficked checkered vinyl floor.

Since I am going to talk about the problems with our system of health care here in the United States and work very hard to build a case for a more proactive and personalized model. I thought it important for me to explain

Aleksey

the life-journey that has me look at the world so different from many of my fellow US citizens fortunate enough to be born here. Just a few generations after the first of their kin were processed at Ellis Island.

THE FRUIT HEIST

I was born Aleksey Romanovich Lubarsky, in Moscow Russia towards the end of 1968 and at the height of the USSR prowess. Eventually my parents were able to bribe and fight their way out in 1979 and immigrate through Vienna and then Italy. Finally arriving in the city that never sleeps where I have been living ever since. Although, it was one of the few times in the history of the evil empire, that the iron curtain was lifted high enough to let a relatively small group of people out. My wife's family, in fact, were refused exit by the Soviet authorities and ended up staying another decade before they were finally able to leave with just the clothes on their back. During that time, her parents were mostly treated as pariahs, traitors, and enemies of the state. They had to forfeit their jobs as engineers and find work wherever they could to sustain themselves. Alina was just a child then but by her sixteenth birthday she was very clear that she was going to leave the Soviet Union for freer shores no matter what. When we met here in New York she was a fiery eighteen-year-old, with big dreams, wide eyes, and unshakable determination.

On some level, growing up in the Soviet Union was perhaps no different than growing up anywhere else. Most adults there knew very little of the outside world, and as children we had no idea at all, and had nothing to compare it to. We thought running around the neighborhood playing with sticks from the woods and cans from the garbage was normal. We traded gum wrappers as if they were gold coins and played with coat buttons in leu of marbles. Got into fights. Found ourselves on the painful side of a homemade slingshot. Sprayed each other with water out of spray bottles when the temperature was below freezing. Picked up cigarette butts on the streets of Moscow and then tried to smoke them in the bushes.

Asked strangers for change and bought trinkets and ice cream.

After a thorough investigation of where I got the colorful guitar pin, I was wearing on my lapel, my mom walked me back to the kiosk where I bought it and made me return the ill-gotten gain.

When I was about 5 years old, construction crews came and dug up all the sewage pipes on our street leaving dozens of man-size piles of hardened refuge throughout the front yard of the four-story walk-up complex that were a more ghetto version of the projects I later visited in Brooklyn's Flatbush area. All the kids climbed and rummaged through those man-made hills looking for anything shiny or valuable, someone accidentally flushed down the main pipe that they could scavenge. Honestly, I'm a little disappointed that after all that toxic exposure I did not develop some kind of superpower, like Bruce Banner of the Incredible Hulk fame.

There was always a drunk or two sprawled out on the staircase that I'd have to step over as I came home from school with a key around my neck. As a rare treat, I would join all of Moscow, and drink from the same thick transparent glass tumbler, set on a vending machine that dispensed sparkling water for a penny, and a sweeter browner version for three. On one memorable occasion, the doorbell rang in our tiny apartment. When I opened the door, pulling the handle with both hands, there in front of me, was a giant, real life Santa Clause. I could not believe my eyes. He was dressed in a red suit with white trim. Black boots, thick belt around his large waist, silver buckles, a huge red bag over his shoulder, and a clip board in his hand. "Are you Aleksey", he slurred, staring intently at the list in front of him. Da! I answered. To that he handed me a small toy car, and stumbled away, towards the parked sled.

I think.

Once, the police came to our apartment and took my parents in for questioning, because a bunch of us kids found a truck parked in front of one of the buildings with some boxes of oranges in the back. We took a few and ate them as we walked home. Some of the guys decided to go back for more and were caught, and in true proletariat fashion they had to rat out anyone who had anything to do with the fruit heist. Of course, they mentioned my name. I remember my mom saying to my dad, and in hushed tones, that if fruit was more readily available, we would have never stolen them.

I was let off with a warning.

The only time I remember my mother being really mad with me is when I got home from school one day and found no one there except my younger brother. I was seven and he was four. We were both hungry. So, I walked him over to the bus stop nearby and we rode on the pre-war public transport for about 20 minutes to where I remembered my grandmother lived. Eventually when my mom finally tracked us down, well, let's just say that moment stands out vividly, and corporally, in my muscle memory. But that was not unusual for children of that time and place, as we would disappear into the woods across the street from where we lived till it got dark most days. And came home only when we were either starving or frozen.

A famous story my father loves to tell is when he sent me to a store a couple of blocks away to buy mayonnaise as they were getting ready to entertain some family and friends. When I came back, I had a large piece of meat, wrapped in butcher paper, slung over my arms. I explained that although they did not have mayonnaise, they did have this nice piece of meat at a good price.

I was 3 at the time.

The schools in the Soviet Union were very strict. We wore identical blue uniforms and showed tremendous reverence for the teachers. There were busts of Lenin and Stalin all over the school and red banners with different 'always be ready' type sayings hung on the walls. During the Red October ceremony for the children in our school, it was I, already a young Pioneer with a red 'pionersky galstuk' (tie/scarf) around my neck, who proudly pinned the five-point star with Lenin's childhood likeness at the center, on my six-year-old brothers' lapel. Named after Yuri Gagarin, the first man in space and the heartthrob of the USSR, this kid was blessed with good looks, an artist's sensitivity, and an uproarious way of looking at the world.

COMING TO AMERICA

Fast forward to when we finally arrived at Kennedy Airport, I was 10 years old and vividly recall my fear of not being able to speak the language or get along with the other children of this foreign land. Once I entered the sixth grade at PS 22 in Flushing Queens, it only took about six months for me to speak English relatively fluently. And because, unlike Brighton Beach, that has a dense population of immigrants from the former USSR, there were not many Russian speakers in the area where we lived, and that may be a contributing factor that has me speaking English with virtually no accent today.

At least I don't hear it.

Math came easy to me as I completed the third grade in the Soviet school, where education was much more advanced and rigorous, I'm sorry to say. So I hardly opened a book till about the nineth grade here, as I was already intimately familiar with the rudimentary subject. It was soon after that that my poor studying habits and know-it-all attitude caught up with me as I was introduced to geometry and algebra in the nineth grade. From that moment on my interest in the formal scholastic part of my life faded.

By the time I was 13 my dad had about 10 yellow cabs that he owned, as well as a one-story building on seventeenth street, used as an auto repair shop to maintain the rapidly growing fleet. Everything was of course leveraged on top of each other and any cashflow he generated quickly went to pay the many mortgages that were constantly shrieking like baby vultures at feeding. A few days a week and on weekends I would take the train to west seventeenth street, to help keep the place clean, do light repairs, and learn how the business worked.

Honestly, never before or the many years since, have I seen anyone work as hard as my dad, with my mom always by his side. Recently he joked that he would put in 8 days per week, as he showed up a day early. And that is hardly an exaggeration, as he came to work for the morning shift before 5 am and did not get home till 9 pm most days including the weekend.

Sometimes getting up in the middle of the night to rescue one of his stranded taxis on the dark and mostly empty streets of New York City.

Once he took me along on one of these midnight rescue missions, put me behind the wheel of a broken-down yellow cab we found in Brooklyn and pushed me with his car all the way to the west side of Manhattan. I probably don't need to tell you that if a car does not start there is no power steering or power breaks, so my teenage body got the work out of a lifetime, as he screamed out instructions out of his open window, 'left, right, slow down!"

Unfortunately, this remarkable work ethic, and 'failure is not an option' attitude, which was innate to my dad, also came with some less healthy habits that he brought here from the communist eutopia we left behind. To get anything done there you had to know people in high places, and to know people like that, you had to provide them with those things that they consider valuable.

In our politics I believe it's called 'lobbying'.

I shared this story in much more detail in my last book, "*The Art of Selling The Art of Healing: How the Rebels of Today are Creating the Healthcare of Tomorrow and Why Your Life Depends on It*" so I'll highlight it here slightly to share the journey that brought me to this paradigm. When I was 16, my dad was detained by two NYC detectives for bribing a state official. So, I had to take over the family business with a fleet of 24 yellow cabs, two tow trucks, an auto repair and body shop on west forty-seventh street. With some 60 hardnosed, and super diverse and eccentric drivers, managers, mechanics, as well as hundreds of customers.

It seems the agents who oversaw the Taxi and Limousine Commission in NYC were less receptive to my father's generous 'lobbying' overtures than the KGB back home and awarded him a 3–5-year sentence in an upstate prison, out of the 15-year maximum that he could have received. Interestingly, he could have avoided all the drama simply by surrendering some of the brass from this government agency who were the actual targets of this crackdown. He refused. When the arresting officer found out he was so impressed that he bought my father lunch.

So, while he was there, I ran his business for some three years, getting the real-world education of my life, till he finally came back and took the proverbial wheel. By that time there was no going back, and I ended up opening an auto repair shop in the west village on the corner of Seventh Avenue South and Carmine Street. Over the next few years, we built that business into a thriving and well-known classic car center that specialized in antique English cars like the Cigar Jaguar, MGB, and the beautiful Triumph TR6, a two-seat convertible that I first bought for $125 and restored to its original glory.

When I was 25, the man who owned the property of the shop where I worked, filed for bankruptcy. This was primarily because of the early 1990's recession that affected many people in new car sales, real estate, and construction. And while it officially ended in March of 1991, the labor market continued to contract for years after and trickled down to every other industry and small business. We had a five-year balloon mortgage on the land and building, and planned to take ownership after that time, but the Resolution Trust Corporation (RTC) a government owned asset management company took all his properties, and put them into one, multi-million-dollar pool. I stayed there for another couple of years in limbo, coasting on the momentum created over the last five years, and one fine morning the US marshals came and padlocked the building.

Driving home that somber day, I had the office computer on the back seat of my fancy car with over 10,000 client contacts that I had serviced over the years, and some of the signed headshots of the more famous people I met who lived in the area. My son was about two at the time, and I quickly realized that without that shop, and the technicians who worked there, I had no marketable skills that would allow me to get a regular job like most of the people I knew had.

BACK TO THE USSR

One of my dad's younger partners became pretty affluent after the fall of the Soviet Union, as he was head of a large collective farm complex that was privatized, and he was given first dibs to buy the whole thing for pennies on the ruble. He lived not too far away from me here in NY part of the year, and we were kind of friends as he was just a few years older. After one of our morning racquet ball games, he suggested that I go to work for 'the corporation' headquartered in proximity to the Kremlin. My father's closest friend, from his early years as a taxi driver in Moscow, became super wealthy as well, having built one of the largest companies at the time that purchased sunflower seeds from all over Russia, turned it into oil, and then sold it by the shipload around the world.

My job would be to canvas the countryside, and sell farmers on contracting the harvest with us, and for that I would earn a generous commission. When my wife first heard of this idea, and saw my enthusiasm for it, she sobbed like a child. I did not see it as clearly, but had I made that move, I would have probably made lots of money, drank lots of vodka, and had lots of fun, but would most likely end up forfeiting my young family.

The other option was to work with a relative of mine. This guy was about 7 years my senior and one of the most difficult and unpleasant people I've ever met. And that's saying something. But he was talking to me for a few years about going into the medical business. He was working for a psychiatrist with a heavy accent, and limp handshake who did psychological testing In medical offices on people who were involved in vehicle or work-related accidents. At first, I would just come to the office and help patients fill out what was a 30-page psychological assessment, that helped the lawyer build a case, as I later understood.

It wasn't difficult work, and I got to do what I really liked and was naturally good at, speaking with different people and being of service to them. One lady who came to the office without her glasses needed me to read the entire test to her, as she answered yes or no to the many questions. One particular question that I asked stays with me as one of those moments that's easy to recall in vivid detail. Do you consider yourself attractive, I read off the sheet without much thought or eye contact. No. She answered as a matter-of-factly. I can still picture her kind face and those deep dark eyes, and could not disagree more, although I said nothing.

After a few months of working in different offices around New York's more 'up-and-coming" neighborhoods, I told my relative that we should open our own company since we're already familiar with how the system worked. After he overcame his initial hesitation, we formed an LLC, rented an office, hired a team of PhD psychologists, contracted with a testing company in Arizona, and went to work selling our program to medical centers in Brooklyn, Queens, and The Bronx.

Within six months checks started flowing from insurance companies large and small at a rate that was thrilling and slightly concerning. It was like pulling the handle on a slot machine and having all the lights and bells go off as shiny gold coins begin to fall all over the floor and around your feet. After about a year into this business, however, having invested a significant sum of money into the partnership, I got a closer look at how the sausage was made, and honestly, it made me queasy.

You'd think someone who left the dirt, cold, and noise of an auto repair business and entered 'health care' would be happy to work in a clean office, talk on the phone, and periodically take money to the bank. But I was stressed, as I tried to walk through a minefield of corruption and sidestep shady characters with a gangster aura who liked to yell at the top of their lungs to make some evil point. Spraying the air in bursts of saliva every time they used a word with a 'th, p, or f' sound. My partner on the other hand was in his element and would call me out on what he considered cowardice to do what was necessary. Once yelling across the entire office, frightening the half-dozen employees who tried to become invisible and blend in with their workstations, that my unwillingness to do the hard things was why he was so much more successful than me.

Eventually we decided to part company as our personalities, goals, and risk threshold did not align.

During this separation process he vindictively refused to release the funds that we agreed belonged to me, just a few weeks after my wife and I made a downpayment, and signed the contract for a house that we would never be able to afford without that money. He was sitting at the dining room table, in our otherwise empty new home, when he nonchalantly broke the devastating news.

They say that stress is the number one contributor to many of our current health problems, and I can attest to this, because not long after the pivotal moment when I found myself sitting across the table from my partner and relative that my own health troubles began. I went to sleep that night, or the night after, and when I woke up in the morning, I had something that felt like a stroke. A sharp electric pain shot down the left side of my body and inflamed what's called the ring toe on my left foot to twice its normal size. And shortly after that all the other symptoms of psoriatic arthritis began to manifest.

Within a year of that infamous meeting, my ex-partner was indicted by the FBI, and then immediately disappeared. It was a few days later someone found his lifeless body in an out of the way motel. His face bloated and distorted from all the pills he took to end his own life. Obviously, I take no pleasure in this, and when giving the eulogy in front of his children, family, and friends who packed the large room of this old funeral home, I barely kept myself together.

HIGHWAY TO HEALTH

Eventually we settled into a new office and continued to provide a more friendly and gentle psychological testing service for some of the more professional medical centers and attorneys around New York. By then I had met many terrific doctors who were unique in their philosophy and approach to life as they were actually in the business of helping people get well. They had much less interest in profits or marketing, they just wanted to practice the ancient craft of helping people restore optimal function by identifying the underlying cause and addressing it directly.

Sadly, I've come to find this to be a self-defeating quality with most doctors who run their own practices, as many of them tend to be altruistic to a fault. They sincerely want to help people get well in a system designed to manage established disease for the duration of the medical consumer's life. Literally criminalizing anyone who would dare question the system and try to help people escape the disease management matrix. Perhaps that is one reason why, when I meet a doctor who got in trouble with the system, I give them every benefit of the doubt.

Once I saw how authentically selfless these doctors were, and how deeply they believed in what they did, I wanted to share their message with others and hopefully bring some clients into their offices. So, I started a radio show called 'Highway to Health'. It was on a local AM station 1240 WGBB, founded in 1922 it was one of the first broadcasting stations in the nation, and the very first on Long Island.

I spent over 10 years interviewing some of the most brilliant doctors, authors, and celebrities from around the world. But it was after the first year that I clearly saw the sizable cracks in the concrete veil that was placed over my eyes as it regards health and health care.

Like everyone else, I knew that the way you spell relief is R.O.L.A.I.D.S. I knew that if you had a stomachache or acid indigestion, you need the plop, plop, fiz, fiz, oh what a relief it is, antacid. Of course, when you have a cold then, and as everyone knows, it's the nighttime, sniffling, sneezing, coughing, aching, stuffy head, fever so you can rest medicine. But I never saw a commercial that said, 'the power that made the body heals the body'. No one told me that health comes from the inside out not outside in. And that your headache is probably not the result of an aspirin deficiency. In all my years I've never heard that processed white sugar was poison, other than from an elderly art teacher in seventh grade who had us draw a bag of sugar depicted as an evil character.

For the most part we are living in a world we cannot see and get angry when someone points it out.

After about a year of interviewing these doctors and taking on a few sponsors, I organized a breakfast meeting where a couple of the doctors shared their unique philosophy and approach to care. And then what happened amazed me, as the sponsors and guests who attended this intimate event became clients of the doctors I introduced. So, if nothing else, I clearly saw that I was not completely delusional. Because when reasonable people hear logical concepts, even the kind that fly in the face of those they may have been indoctrinated with their entire life, they shed those limiting beliefs like the survivors of Jonestown after witnessing the inherent dangers of "drinking the cool aid".

THE LONG JOURNEY HOME

As I was driving home that final day, leaving behind the auto-repair business I had spent the last eight years of my life building, my mind was racing as to what I could do to provide for my young family. I could not easily get an entry level job with my lack of pedigree and abundance of boss energy. Even though I tried applying for a few positions like car sales, cold caller, waiter, and pharmaceutical sales, of all things. All unsuccessful, and one older man who was interviewing me, got offended about something I said or the way I said it, his face turned beet red, and he kicked me out. So, entrepreneurship is the only thing I know, and had to stumble around like a miner in a pitch-black low sealing tunnel for years before I honed my Spidey reflexes, and my soft hands became more callous with experience.

Over the last thirty years, I developed a unique ability to take unlikely business ideas off the ground and grow them into successful enterprises. When I first started building conferences, I did it by taking out loans on my many credit cards and then working as hard as I could to leverage those resources and engage as many people as possible by phone, mail, and in person. I spent the last 15 years building a thriving conference business, and it was the government lock downs this time, as the US marshals the last, that brough all that effort and investment to an abrupt end.

But we are not the kind of people to dwell on the past, complain, and cry in our soup. We take a little time for reflection, sit down and draw up a new approach. One based on all the past experiences and revelations that allowed me to become the man I am today, which is so different from the innocent and credulous boy I once was.

TO FLATTEN A CURVE

In early March of 2020, I was hosting a dinner event for about 50 doctors, many of whom were scheduled to speak at our two-day conference in May of that year. By then my team and I spent four months building this event. We booked one of the largest hotel ball rooms on Long Island, contracted our keynote speakers, printed and mailed some 30,000 magazines, along with 750,000 direct mail flyers. We planned ads that would run on the radio and television, as well as numerous publications like the NYT and the WSJ. We had about 150 exhibiting companies, along with some 80 doctors and experts flying in from around the country.

This was quite the production to say the least.

As I was greeting people in the lobby of one of my favorite restaurants on that March evening, many of the doctors would not shake my hand, because by that time whispers of a possible pandemic began to grow in scope and volume. For the most part I dismissed it as I have every other overhyped threat I've witnessed over the years. From SARS, N1H1, MERS, the bird flu, and ZIKA to name a few. The last one was supposedly most threating in Puerto Rico. But after each of my conferences I have something of a ritual as I take the first plane on Monday morning after the weekend event, and I fly out to Isla Verde in San Juan. There is a small boutique hotel near one of the most perfect beaches in the world where I spend about four days playing in the surf, baking in the sun, and reading spy novels. Of course, because of the perceived threat that was trumpeted on every news station; the plane, the hotel, and beach were mostly empty which was just perfect for me.

I don't take these threats very seriously, is what I'm trying to say. And you may think that this attitude is throwing caution to the wind, but at this point I've heard the experts cry wolf so many times that for the most part

I hardly take notice when they bellow and howl about the next end of the world event. And because I've turned off the news many years ago, it may very well be that I'll meet my end because of some world consuming catastrophe, or serial killer, but somehow, I imagine it to be much less eventful when the time actually comes. Primarily because human nature tends to concern itself with existential worries that for the most part never come to pass, and at the same time close their eyes to those that are statistically damming, and as common as white sugar, pesticides, and vegetable oils.

Perhaps that's one reason we've never seen a horror film where some obese guy, with full blown diabetes, was just sitting there, eating donuts by the dozen and with both hands, while shooting back cans of soda for two hours.

The End.

Not long after the two weeks of flattening the curve, it was clear that my upcoming conference and my entire business in fact, were going to be the collateral damage of this hysterical overreaction and tyrannical dictate. The months that followed were filled with sadness, doubt, stress, and trepidation as I once again found myself without a business or prospects for what to do next.

SEE YOU AT THE TOP

At five am on the cold morning of December 12, 1993, it was still dark, and the parking lot of the Westbury Music Fair mostly empty. I was sitting in my car fully awake, dressed in a suit and tie, waiting for the early meeting with my mentor and guru, Zig Ziglar.

Before I became interested in trying to understand how to resolve the underlying cause of my chronic illness, and the inner workings of our system of health care, ostensibly driven by that mission. I was very interested in personal-development and becoming successful and perhaps even wealthy in the American free-enterprise system. So, I followed some of the top names in that industry around the country, like a dedicated student of a kung fu master. Attending events that featured speakers like Tony Robins, author of *Awaken the Giant Within*, Mark Victor Hansen, creator of the *Chicken Soup for the Soul* series, Mary Lou Retton, an Olimpic Champion once considered the most famous woman in America, and Brian Tracy, author of *Eat That Frog*. As well as Donald Trump, who at the time was just an author of *The Art of The Deal*, and successful real estate developer and negotiator.

One of the things that I learned from Zig Ziglar, was that "If you help enough other people get what they want, you will automatically get what you want." I am still a strong believer in this philosophy, and it has been a driving force in how I conduct my affairs. If you wish to be successful, find people who you can help succeed. If you want to be happy, bring joy to others. And if you want to be healthy or regain optimal function, here as well, this somewhat counterintuitive approach seems just as effective.

Towards the end of 2019, after fifteen years of effort and tremendous financial investment, I was certain that I found my life calling. Organizing conferences that focus on bringing cutting edge approaches in the art and science of human optimization, to the huddled masses yearning to breathe free, and be well. My goal was to establish these two-day conferences around the nation, write books, and interview the leaders of this movement.

But you know what they say, 'man plans and GD laughs.'

So, as I sat in stunned and meditative silence during that first shuttered year, the thought came to me that perhaps it's not showcasing the leaders in human optimization, but actually designing a system to deliver this kind of proactive and personalized approach to care, was my true calling. So once the lockdowns were ended by decree and the mandates lifted by fiat, I did not rush back to try and resuscitate my beloved conference business.

Last year, I organized a relatively small dinner-meeting with just a couple of my doctors, and our ScHO Keynote Carol Alt, the supermodel, bestselling author, and renowned actress with a Doctorate in Alternative Health Studies who spoke on the topic of "One Woman's Guide to Moving

Mountains" to a full house and rave reviews. There I introduced, via power point presentation, our Science of Human Optimization model of care. One that will hopefully focus some of the greatest minds in functional medicine and help a million people get to the root cause of chronic symptomatology, circumvent many of the modern health problems that we're told are inevitable and incurable, and create structures for optimal, lifelong function, ageless beauty, and youthful longevity.

∾

FINAL THOUGHT

"To be yourself in a world that is constantly trying to make you something else is the greatest accomplishment". – Ralph Waldo Emerson

Chapter Three

LIFESPAN

You thought you were getting free health care, but
actually, you donated your body to science.

Throughout this book I'm going to work hard to answer some of the
following questions. How do we extend human lifespan as much as
possible? How do we condense the diseases of aging into a much smaller
window? How do we design a system of care that aims to resolve chronic
health issues at the root, and works to help us function at the very peak
level of health expression, in the moment, and for the duration of our
vibrant, productive, and fulfilling lives?

But before we talk about creating a better system of health care, I thought
it may be fun to explore some of the inherent problems with this one. And
there are many, but here are a few that I'd like to highlight.

First, the system is almost entirely focused on the indefinite management
of chronic disease. Second, the only time your doctor can access the money
you've paid into your health insurance, is once you already have a well-
established, diagnosable, and chronic disease state. Third, at almost five
trillion dollars per year, growing exponentially, the system is unsustainable
by any measure, but worse, it turned our sickness and disease into a
modern-day gold rush.

Four, the system is fragmented.

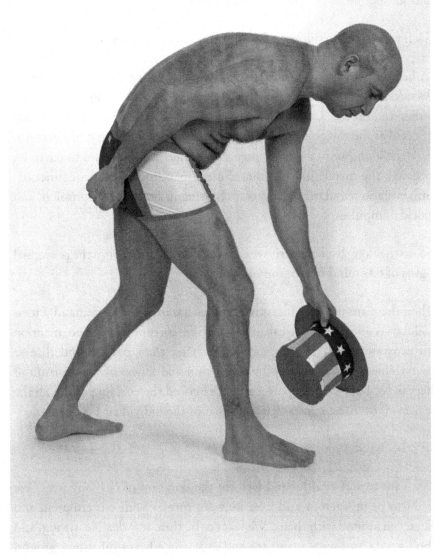

Broken

So, you have your oncologist, once you develop cancer. An endocrinologist, once you're diagnosed with diabetes. A rheumatologist once you have arthritis. A cardiologist, once you develop heart disease. And then of course you have your neurologist, who's going to help diagnose your early onset Alzheimer's. In fact, according to the American Association of Medical Colleges (AAMC) there are more than 135 medical specialties and subspecialties available for future doctors to consider.

Each requiring a residency of between three and eight years.

In her wonderful book *Good Energy: The Surprising Connection Between Metabolism and Limitless Health,* Casey Means, MD along with her co-writer and brother Calley Means, talks about how her mental health was affected as she was going through rigorous surgical residency. She explains how the high-pressure environment, low-value nutrition, and unrelenting pedal-to-the-metal lifestyle contributed to mitochondrial disfunction, inflammation, and oxidative stress resulting in brain fog, depression, and suicidal impulses.

So, to that long list of experts we can add a psychiatrist, once the proverbial lights of our mind flicker and dim.

Then there are perverse incentives, moral hazards, elastic demand, cross-industry collusion, political and scientific corruption, not to mention an ecosystem that focuses on profit rather than people, and disease management rather than optimal function and longevity. The pursuit of happiness, I am sad to report, for those behind the curtain pulling all the leavers, is in direct contradiction to that of the individual US citizen.

In other words, you, and me.

We want to stay healthy and well for the duration of our long lives. We want to be prosperous and free; we want to play with our children, and later, run around with theirs. We want to be thin, stay flexible, strong, and look good. And we want to see and experience beautiful things around the planet as we continue to enrich this remarkable experience called life.

They, on the other hand, want a piece of that almost five trillion-dollar disease management pie, and for that to happen, you need to be chronically ill, subservient, and dumb.

In fact, during the founding of this nation, Benjamin Rush, signer of the Declaration of Independence, physician and political leader, said that *"unless we put medical freedom into the constitution the time will come when medicine will organize into an undercover dictatorship to restrict the art of healing to one class of men and deny equal privileges to others."*

Perhaps if it was not clear before, maybe the tyrannical lockdowns, and treacherous mandates of 2020-2022 showed us, just how brilliantly prescient he was.

PERVERSE INCENTIVES

Running for third base full out, the junior league slugger falls face first onto the ground and remains still for what seems like an eternity. His parents, watching from the stands, jump up with shocked concern, and within a few seconds the dad has his unconscious son in his hands sprinting towards the car so that he can drive the boy to a local emergency room.

Frightening scenario for any parent, and one difficult to have a rational conversation around. Turns out, as the plot of John Q. unfolds, Michael, the 10-year-old son of John Quincy Archibald, played by Denzel Washington, desperately needed a heart transplant. The cost associated with this procedure in the 1990's was around $250,000 ($1.6 million today) and the HMO's ... the callous health insurance gestapo, were unwilling to cover the procedure. Additionally, there is a wait list for donated organs that must go through multiple steps to be considered a match.

Without giving away the plot, in case you wanted to see a propaganda film for socialized medicine. John takes the law into his own hands and bends public will, and providence herself, to achieve what seemed impossible. But let us take a step back here, cool our righteous indignation, and have a cordial and thoughtful discussion about a difficult and emotional topic.

Should health care be free?

Of course, you say! Health care is a human right and therefore any civilized society must provide unlimited and immediate access to anyone who needs care, free of charge and ad infinitum. Or perhaps more accurately, paid for by a third party, like the government, or the health insurance company. Which of course is ultimately paid by everyone who pays taxes and premiums. But it really does not matter who will be responsible to pay this bill, as long as everyone understands that it cannot, and it won't be the quintessential *me*. Which is the attitude of those eccentric characters who finger paint signs that say "healthcare is a human right". "Single payer NOW!" and scream at protests demanding, the Easter Bunny deliver on his promise. In spite of reality or the laws of physics, somehow, we must organize the government and warlocks so that the services of highly trained professionals, along with all the very expensive equipment they need to provide care is made available to everyone, forever, and for free.

And I, at least in theory, would wholeheartedly agree.

As a sentient being, a father, grandfather, and someone who has been in health care most of his adult life, the last thing I want to see is another human being suffer needlessly. We must help people whenever we can, it is our moral duty and holy dictate. And once I figure out how to use that authentic Harry Potter Magic Wond that my daughter left behind after she grew up and moved to her own place, perhaps I can find the corresponding incantation to bring this fantasy to life. Outside of that unlikely scenario, we live in a world of limited resources. Be that time, money, seats in an emergency room, or available organs that match our blood type. So those resources must be allocated in a way where they go to the areas of society they are needed most.

The best way we as humans found to allocate those scarce resources in most areas of our society is through the imperfect model of capitalism. Prices, in fact, is how we do that. When something we need or want goes up in price, we buy less of it, when the price goes down, we may buy more. The cost of an item or service is directly affected by the availability of natural resources. The cost of diesel, salary of the truck driver, and perhaps a million other factors.

No, you say. Capitalism, to fairly allocate scarce resources, when it's a matter of life and death?!! Unacceptable. "Single Payer NOW!!" they start chanting.

One of the most impressive approaches to allow the free market back into healthcare that I've seen so far is through the Health Savings Accounts (HSA) signed into law as part of a larger Medicare Modernization Act by Jeorge W. Bush in 2003. It allowed the individual person to place pre-tax money aside and if used for health-related services it would literally double their purchasing power. Employers can also add funds to those accounts as incentives, and if someone was struggling financially, and needed access to care then perhaps charities, or worst-case scenario, the government can contribute to the person's HSA. For more expensive emergencies, the HSA comes with a catastrophic policy that kicks in after the deductible is met, and then all the expenses are covered. This seems like a practical and effective way to place more responsibility for health care in the hands of the individual, reduce expenses, and improve outcomes.

So here is the sad and practical trouble with offering limitless health care to anyone who needs it free of charge. First, just because you give a health insurance card to 40 million people who did not have one before, does not mean they have any more meaningful access to the static number of doctors, hospitals, or band aids. All these scarce resources must be shared among those new members as well as the 290 million original ones. So, if the wait in your local emergency room was 6 hours before, now it may just as easy be 8 or 10. With a large percentage of the people leaving in frustration before being seen.

If I once had to wait a month to see a specialist now it may be three or four or six.

Socialism is equality at the level of poverty; in every society it's implemented over the last century of the bloodiest years of human history. While in healthcare, it manifests as penurious levels of wellbeing, escalation of chronic disease, out of control cost, and third-world access to the system that is ostensibly there to stave off the tide of this lifestyle inflicted pandemic.

The allocation of limited resources will either be done by the market, mandates, or rationing. Either way the outcome is the same. And I would argue, giving access to free health care makes it less fair. As you would need to depend on who you know, who you can bribe or, as in John Q. scenario, who you can force to do your bidding against their will.

As a matter of fact, perhaps that movie is the perfect analogy of how socialized medicine ultimately works.

THE BROKEN HEART MILL

But, ok. Let's for a moment imagine that we can somehow escape reality, suspend belief, wave that magic wand while incanting "Wingardium Leviosa" and pretend that we can give a heart to anyone who needs it, and a mysterious benefactor will cover the million-dollar cost of doing this miraculous procedure. Certainly, for the over 750 thousand people who died from heart related illness in the United States last year this would be quite the miracle.

Here we are in this elaborate surgical theater with all the latest and best technology. A great team of world experts who can now replace a heart in under an hour (using robotics and artificial intelligence} rather than the 4-6 hours in years past. It's kind of like a heart transplantation factory, the success rate is 99.8%, the recovery is exceptionally fast because of advances in pharmaceutical development. And the cost is no longer a concern of the person lying on the operating table.

It's a beautiful scenario and we should savor it if but for a moment.

But what happens now that there is an unlimited supply of organs and the money to pay for the transplantation flows like a proverbial river? Well, what happens to the average person who wins the mega-lottery? It gets them to do what they normally would not. It disrupts the natural ecosystem within their network of friends and family. They buy things they would not otherwise buy and behave in a way that is motivated by the perverse incentives that come with the unnatural financial windfall.

Similarly, when an artificial financial tsunami is experienced by people in the medical field, or any field for that matter, they will behave consistent with the stimulus. Working towards the rewards associated with the service they offer on an unprecedented level. So, as soon as you do a heart transplant, a cool million dollars hits the bank account. Now instead of finding ways to provide care to people in desperate need, the system desperately needs people to provide care to, and feed the ravenous machine.

For example, in 1999 the South Korean government funded a national screening service for thyroid cancer allocating generous resources to the program. A kind and altruistic idea that inadvertently perpetuated an unprecedented number of people tested who presented no symptoms. Resulting in a 15% rise in cancer case diagnosis. So now the smallest lump or bump demanded extreme intervention and invasive biopsies because of the invisible claw of perverse incentive dictates.

In his terrific book *The Price We Pay: What Broke American Health Care – And How to Fix It*, Marty Makary, MD, a cancer surgeon, and Professor of health policy, goes on a national tour to try and understand the problems with the current almost five trillion-dollar bureaucracy known as the United States system of 'health' care. In the very first chapter he comes out swinging as he presents a Baltimore cardiologist who received a great deal of negative media attention for placing unnecessary heart stents in hundreds of patients.

He goes on to discuss doctors who perform vascular surgery, stenting, and lasering harmless plaques in leg arteries with zero regard for necessity, patient, or system. Driven by the more profitable code rather than an actual need. As the Soviets used to say: find me the man and I'll give you the crime. Today, in this medical paradigm it's: bring me a body and we'll find the most profitable procedure. On the one hand we could say that this outlier is just the despicable behavior by a one out trusted medical professional, and on the other, the consistent and natural human expression to do what is ultimately in their own best interest, twisted by an unnatural, and indeed perverse incentive.

OPERATION SPINAL CAP

To put a finer point on it, Michael Drobot, owner of the Pacific Hospital in Long Beach, CA is serving five years in federal prison and must pay a ten million dollar fine for his role in an elaborate scheme to the tune of 950 million dollars in unnecessary surgeries, counterfeit spinal hardware, and bribery. Working in collusion with Ron Calderon (D), the California State Senator, who received payoffs to keep this scheme going, and who is also serving a well-deserved prison sentence. This group funneled forty million dollars to 'runners', as well as doctors, to procure people for surgery regardless of need. Once the cheap screws were surgically implanted in a victim's spine for anywhere from $350,000 to $450,000 per procedure and paid for by some third party. Who could then question if the operation was necessary or be willing to remove and examine the authenticity of the materials used.

And if you're like me, you may ask, how much can a pedicle screw cost, that you would need to get a counterfeit option, while charging half a million dollars for the procedure? Would it not make logic to actually install the best possible hardware available so as not to bring attention to your criminal enterprise in case of complications and patient complaints?

But sometimes greed makes very smart people very stupid, and when they also happen to think that they are GD then it's euphorically so. When I had my auto repair shop, I once had a person drive up, and tell me that his car kept stalling, and he would need to get a boost to get it started. He recently had his battery and alternator replaced, so it could not be that he assured me. Once my mechanics popped the hood and looked under it, they called me over because they never saw anything quite like it. Indeed, there was a new, albeit cheap generic battery installed, the alternator, however, was spraypainted in place. They did not even bother to remove it, because you could see the silver paint was all over the screws that held it in place, and the belt that drove it. From what I understand he paid about four times more than what we would usually charge to install the best available parts.

But because he was in a desperate situation, he had no choice, and was forced to trust a criminal.

MORAL HAZARDS

Here's a hypothetical. You're a transplant surgeon about to replace a patient's liver. The hospital will invoice the insurance company or some government program $878,400 for this miraculous procedure. Once successfully done, and the patient is in the recovery room surrounded by their emotional, prayerful, and grateful family, you will be treated as a demigod with all the admiration and accolades that come with it.

And, not undeservingly, I'd say.

Now here is the trillion-dollar question, what if that patient's liver can be restored to normal function by adjusting her diet, reducing alcohol consumption, doing a high mineral salt flush, supplementing with glutathione, and perhaps doing a lemon juice, olive oil and cayenne pepper cleanse each morning for a month.

In his terrific book, *100 IS THE NEW 30: How Playing the Symphony of Longevity will Enable us to Live Young for a Lifetime,* Jeffey Gladden, MD, founder of the Gladden Longevity Center in Irving Texas, shares a story about one of his patients whose father died of liver cirrhosis. This person was overweight, with abdominal obesity and insulin resistance. After a recent trip to the gastroenterologist, the doctor asserted that his liver was so damaged that he would most probably need to be placed on a transplant list.

Long story short, after recommending cardio exercise, cleaning up his diet, adding a Berberine supplement as well as drinking tea with Gynostemma pentaphyllum, also known as Jiaogulan, or Southern Ginseng two to three times per day, this man no longer needed a transplant, and miraculously his liver had minimal disease detected.

In the off chance that you as a surgeon, took the time to learn something that can help those people who find their way on to your operating table, restore function to their compromised organ with a simple solution to a complicated problem, rather than the other way around. Would you then lean over and whisper this option in the ear of this sentient ATM? I imagine not. "We did not become surgeons to give dietary advice." Is what one colleague told Casey Means, MD, author of *Good Energy*, after she suggested they implement nutrition as part of the treatment protocol for patients with recuring health issues. And why would the medical schools that train a new generation of doctors to do these complex and expensive procedures, want to teach any of the possible folk remedy solutions that don't involve the opening of your chest cavity with a pair of stainless-steel poultry shears and a crowbar?

So here then is the systemic moral hazard. No matter how honorable you are or noble your intentions, once the machine is set in place, and everyone is thoroughly committed to their role, and is under a tremendous amount of pressure to produce, you may as well install a conveyor belt in that OR. Because eventually everyone in America will get a brand-new liver one that was 3D printed minutes prior in a room down the hall.

We saw a small glimpse of this medical tyranny with the way the covid reaction fiasco played out; simultaneously and on a world-wide scale mind you. Forced lockdowns, mandated medical experimentation, ubiquitous masking, the endless Simon Says games with grouchy-Fauci, as well as that innovative social distancing idea, that some germaphobe in a latex suit imposed on the rest of us. And how the media, politicians, drug manufacturers, and entire medical system worked together in unison, like synchronized swimmers at the Tokyo Olympics, to convince, cajole, manipulate, guilt, bribe, browbeat, and eventually force everyone to do what was, you know, for your own safety.

So, everyone wins.

The hospital pays out its investors handsomely, the doctor gets his impressive salary, the insurance company justifies charging higher premiums, the government raises taxes, the economy expands, and you get a new liver.

For what is ostensibly, absolutely free.

ELASTIC DEMAND

If we placed a mountain of cash in the middle of Times Square, all the way up to that crystal ball that's ceremoniously dropped on New Years Eve, how long would it take before all that money was gone? Similarly, if you pour trillions of dollars into the management of chronic illness, how long will it take for the nation that does this, before it runs out of money and must shut down the government?

There is a word "azart" in Russian that does not seem to have an English counterpart. It describes that feeling of a gambling frenzy, when your eyes get big, the heart is pounding, and there is an adrenalin rush that blocks out everything else on the periphery. All you can think about is placing the next bet and grab at those jackpot winnings that are always just out of reach.

This feeling, much like the qualities of an illicit drug, can be extremely addictive.

Of course, because there are no restrictions to access what is considered a valuable commodity (a mountain of cash in the first rhetorical question) it would disappear as quickly as you could replenish it. And soon as word got out, people from all over the world would fight their way to the center of Manhattan, to grab a handful of Benjamins for themselves. Eventually cutting down all the trees in the world won't provide enough paper for the giant treasury printers to satiate the swarming masses.

A similar "azart" is happening in our system of health care, as those with an entitlement mentality demand that any deterrent or resistance in the form of co-pays or deductibles be removed so they and their comrades can grab a fist full of other people's time and expertise, in the form of free medical care. Unfortunately, as this frenzy continues it becomes inevitable that guards, restraints, and barriers must be placed, as access becomes more restricted, and austerity becomes the norm.

CROSS INDUSTRY COLLUSION

How do the medical industry, the food industry, the government industry, the media industry, and the chemical industry work together to create the most profitable outcome for their shareholders? If you eat more, have more health problems, live in chronic fear for your life, pay more taxes, and take more medications, you are then the model citizen of a government run by mega corporations and puppet criminals.

When you are toxic with the over 80,000 chemicals released into the environment, develop a chronic condition like obesity for example, tune in to the bought-off propogandists who tell you what to do and what to think, and that fat is beautiful and sexy, then you can help bring forth the next trillion-dollar industry by filling the Denmark bank accounts of Novo Nordisk, for their new drug called Ozempic. And, with 60% or our population being pre-diabetic, those accounts will be filled to overflowing by your government representative, who can then justify a new form of creative taxation to pay for it.

POLITICAL AND SCIENTIFIC CORRUPTION

Perhaps there was no way to fix this particular liver and the only way to save the patient is to actually do a transplant. How did we get to the place where this person and many like them damaged their liver to the point of irreversible cirrhosis. Why is Nonalcoholic Fatty Liver Disease (NAFLD) the most common cause of liver transplants for young adults. Could it be, that either by omission or commission, the food pyramid implemented by our political, industrial, and medical leadership, one that recommended eleven servings of grain per day at the very bottom of it as the main food group, and then hung-up posters displaying these directions to perdition in every classroom around the nation.

Perhaps it was this legerdemain that had something to do with an obesity epidemic and the many comorbidities that come along with it. Would it surprise you to learn that 93% of the academics on the USDA panel that designed the 2020 Dietary Guidelines for Americans had conflicts of interest with food companies.

Then the now infamous scandal about the Sugar Research Foundation paying off scientists at Harvard to place the blame for coronary heart disease at the feet of fat and cholesterol in steak and eggs, rather than the actual culprit of sugar and soda. The study, first published in the New England Journal of Medicine in 1965, set the course for the many metabolic problems that continue to damage people's health till this day. Speaking with a Family Nurse Practitioner (FNP) working for a service doing senior home visits in PA, I learned about one of her patients injecting 25,000 units of insulin per day. At the age of 65 this man was dealing with all the health problems associated with barely controlled diabetes. On one of her first visits, she noticed a case of large plastic bottles of black soda with a red label in his kitchen, and asked how often he drank it. "I have a glass of soda and a cupcake as a snack about four times per day" was his nonchalant reply. So, when the National Kidney Foundation says that the average US citizen consumes 152 pounds of sugar per year, with 79 pounds of that in the form of high fructose corn syrup, obviously there is a percentage of the population doing much of the heavy lifting.

If you think back to your sugary breakfast cereals, bagels, pasta, croissants, muffins, packaged bread, pizza, donuts, pop tarts, cakes, cookies, chips, and fast food that you were fed as a child in school and at home, you can clearly see the lugubrious and inevitable outcome of those decisions, speciously made for the benefit of your health and wellbeing. I guess we can be grateful for the magnificent design and impressive resilience of the human body that the damage, on the national scale, is not much worse than it is.

Subsequently they permitted the spraying of deadly chemicals on the wheat and then engineered the historically beautiful and life-giving plant so that it's Roundup ready, a deformed version of its former self. Basically, this modern wheat is genetically modified in such a way as to be resistant to this poisonous neuro toxin. Unfortunately, you and I, not so much. This surreptitious attack on our health and wellbeing started in the early 1960's and is what I believe to be a major contributing factor to many of the health challenges we are dealing with in our cities, communities, schools, and hospitals today.

They chalk it up to gluten sensitivity, but 20 years ago, who was gluten sensitive? Such a tiny percentage of the population that you never heard about it being a thing. Suddenly even Italian restaurants are offering gluten free pasta options on their menu, and if that is not a premonition for the end of days, I don't know what is.

PROVE THEM WRONG

In 1981 the FDA approved the use of Aspartame, discovered by James Schlatter, a chemist and researcher who first identified this artificial sweetener in 1965, one purportedly 200 times sweeter than sugar. As this new experiment unfolded, NutraSweet was introduced into most of the processed food and drinks we find in the middle isles of the supermarket, as it was much cheaper to produce, and provided the sweetness we've come to crave. The trouble with this chemical is that it interferes with the body's ability to shut off the hunger hormones, like leptin, allowing us to become satiated and stop eating. So, we are constantly ravenous, stuffing our mouth with everything we can find in a box, a plastic bag, or aluminum can as if the oral cavity was a refuse compactor, and our stomach an incinerator.

Of course, the story of how this substance was able to get passed the FDA and enter our food supply so quickly and on such a scale is one worthy of investigation. If you simply search for information about Aspartame on

Google (the NPR of search engines) the first page of results will be mostly of positive reviews and PR spin. But should you dig a little deeper you can find some eye-opening and frightening backstory. In a short documentary by Kiana Docherty, "The Forbidden History of Aspartame" she explores the corruption between the pharmaceutical companies with unlimited budgets, who would hire away those in the government responsible for overseeing them and unleash the dogs of hell onto an unsuspecting public.

Then there are vegetable oils that became ubiquitous through all the processed food as well. Chemical concoctions like margarine, originally made from animal fats such as beef fallow, with the purpose of providing a less expensive butter alternative to the armed forces and lower classes during the early nineteenth century in France. Later vegetable oils replaced animal fats to make it less expensive still. Today even mainstream medical centers like the Cleveland Clinic acknowledge that the trans-fat in margarine raises LDL, the bad cholesterol while lowering HDL, making blood platelets stickier and increasing the risk of heart disease, which is the leading cause of death in the United States. Vegetable oils are also high in the omega 6 to 3 ratio and have been shown to increase inflammation, one of the major contributing factors to many chronic disease conditions including autoimmune.

So, when my maternal grandmother made her famous napoleon, she used real butter, real sugar and pure, unadulterated flour. She would serve it on very special occasions as the process of making this heavenly pastry was so time and labor intensive. It would take her a couple of days. With the full unenthusiastic participation of my cranky grandfather. Baking the many layers, mixing the cream, and then lovingly sprinkling the crumbs over the top bringing what would be a gentle, creamy, and unforgettable culinary experience to life. The memory of her in that kitchen, mischievously cutting off a small piece from the imperfect side and giving it to me before I had dinner, still has residual feelings of love when I think of it. Sadly, no one from the next generation within our family thought of getting the recipe, and unfortunately it was lost forever with her passing some 30 years ago.

We've stepped away from those simpler days and are living in a time of mechanized abundance on an industrial scale. And believe me, I am not complaining. What's missing, from my perspective, is someone who can help influence the market to produce those things we may enjoy in moderation, by persuading the manufacturers to improve the quality of the materials that go into them. So, the momentary pleasure does not have to come with a lifetime of suffering.

There are so many other things that may be contributing to the erosion of our national health and lifespan potential. From unfiltered tap water, microwave ovens, amalgam fillings, fluoride, microplastics that permeate every area of our life, radiation from endless diagnostic tests, EMF toxicity from our cell phones, that full-body rotisserie at the airport TSA screening, and food options mostly depleted of nutritional value. Those crucial micronutrients that were available in abundance just a couple of generations back.

Then there is the combining of the unhealthy options to make them downright poisonous. Like microwaving your processed egg muffin and sausage in a Styrofoam container for example. Or placing your cell phone in your brassiere near some very sensitive tissue, as four extremely powerful antennas send and receive over one hundred megabits per second tearing into your DNA like a food processor into a ribeye. Now imagine falling asleep with your phone near your head or on your chest. You've just increased your risk of cancer by like 500%.

But wait there's more.

As depressing as all of this is, the deck is set up against us from the very start. According to the July 15, 2005, Environmental Working Group "Body Burden" report, the umbilical cord of a newborn today contains some 273 different forever chemicals. That is, chemicals made so enduringly well that they will be a part of this universe long after we're all gone, and the sun goes dark. Things like fire retardant, methylmercury, lead, dioxins and other chemicals, with longer and more intimidating sounding names.

Then as soon as a newborn baby enters the world and gets a slap on the buttocks, they turn it into a pin cushion as the administering of the ever-increasing vaccination schedule commences. According to the National Institute of Health, 8.1% of infants and toddlers have a length-for-weight greater than 95 percentiles. Meaning that two-year-olds are becoming obese.

And clearly, it's not because of too much breast milk or too little aerobic exercise.

If you're the average person, I know that you most likely have not given many of these things much thought up until this point. Honestly, I remember those blissful days of my own happy unawareness of this sad and overwhelming topic fondly. The only reason I started perusing all this information is to solve a health problem that everyone was telling me was unsolvable. It was as frustrating as it was infuriating. I was always a positive, can-do kind of person, so when the experts were telling me that I had to accept their depressing interpretation of my chronological disintegration, I became determined to find the answer to its permanent resolution.

Illos Probare Iniuriam, was my motto.

The good news is that you don't need to be a medical doctor to find a permanent resolution to a health problem. In fact, I would argue that it's better if you don't come into this challenge with preconceived notions, and the overly cautious, frustrating perception that looks at the issue from a paradigm of the long-term managing of the problem. This current triage medical system is focused on getting you out of there as fast and inexpensively as possible, rather than taking the time to search for the root cause of the symptom and resolving it permanently.

Seek simple solutions to complicated problems rather than the other way around. And then maybe you can prove them wrong.

VITAMIN SHIPWRECK

A friend of mine was telling me a story about some inexplicable health problems she was dealing with, ones progressively getting worse over time. Bleeding gums, skin that would bruise easily, always exhausted and irritated. She consulted with numerous doctors who prescribed one size fits all solutions from their own narrow approach and symptom management paradigm.

The general practitioner said it was all in her mind, the psychiatrist offered antidepressants, the pain specialist, oxycodone. Turns out she was depleted in vitamin C and was developing early stages of scurvy. And perhaps these medical professionals can be forgiven, as we have not seen much of this disease of malnutrition since the sailors of old would succumb to it on their long journeys, subsisting on pickles and beer for months on end. But she did not like or consume any of the citrus fruit known for their vitamin C content, and since the body does not make this essential vitamin, the perfect environment evolved for what is a virtually unheard of, self-inflicted disease of nutritional deficiency.

In fact, Dr. Joel Wallach, ND author of *Dead Doctors Don's Lie*, who worked as a veterinarian pathologist traveling around the world trying to understand the environmental factors in the cause of death of lions, and tigers, and bears. Having performed some 20,000 autopsies on zoo animals, and later 2000 humans, documenting his findings in numerous textbooks, he said the following:

"When an animal or human dies of natural causes, they die of a nutritional deficiency disease."

In one of his books, he talks about a particularly interesting mouse experiment. It seems that for a long-time lab-mice were fed a diet of carrots and cabbage and would usually live 4-6 months which is their normal lifespan in nature. No one can possibly know how many nutrients can be found in any particular batch of vegetables, because we have no idea about the health or mineral content of the soil where they grew. Once some bright scientists designed a pellet that included all the vital nutrients the little guys needed for optimal function, the average lifespan increased fourfold, and they lived an extraordinarily long time.

How many other chronic conditions stem from a deficiency of some important vitamin and mineral? We know that with vitamin D for example, if it's under 20 nanograms per milliliter (ng/mL) you have a much higher chance of developing osteomalacia, which is a weakening of the bones, but you also have a 75% chance of developing colon cancer. That's a 75% chance of developing colon cancer if your vitamin D is under 20 ng/mL for an extended period. But if you are the average person going to an average doctor you probably have no idea of your levels of this crucially important pre-hormone. If you'd like a more thorough understanding of this foundational nutrient, I encourage you to check out some of the presentations by the brilliant and incorruptible Alex Vazquez, who has three doctoral degrees, is the chief editor of the International Journal of Human Nutrition, and Functional Medicine, and writes 1200-page textbooks on optimization and longevity.

Usually when I meet people and they ask me what it is that I do, and after I share my elevator pitch, I ask if they know their vitamin D level. For the most part people have no idea, and in the off chance that they do, the numbers are always extremely low. I was speaking with a close friend of mine to whom I posed this question, and she told me that the last time they checked, her level was a frightening and incomprehensible 4 ng/mL. When I explained the correlation between low vitamin D and increased risk of colon cancer, she told me that she lost her grandmother, aunt, and a few cousins to that same horrific disease. So, we can interpret that as her unfortunate family history, and lamentable genetics that are responsible for this tragic outcome. But perhaps if her family would just supplement with an inexpensive vitamin, and spend a bit more time in the sunshine, without lathering themselves with a sunscreen made from the hormone disrupting oxybenzone and such, the results would have been somewhat less sinister I imagine.

The body needs some 90 essential nutrients to be able to create the next generation of healthy, resilient and buoyant cells. And when you think about it, at least theoretically. If the foundation of our very existence, the cell, has everything it needs to continue making strong, vibrant, and youthful offspring, then perhaps we can age slower and live longer. Much longer. And then if we remove some of the toxicity responsible for damaging the DNA strand then maybe we can circumvent those diseases of our civilized society that we've come to accept as the natural part of aging.

GREAT INVESTMENT

Had I asked about your financial plan for retirement, I'm sure you would tell me how hard you've worked, the education you invested in, the advisors you have, and the savings and investment plan you follow to achieve your goal of enjoying your golden years without having to worry about outliving your money. But how come not one of us has been taught to proactively invest in our life-energy so that when we have all the time and money in the world, we are not hooked up to life-sustaining machines, prostrating ourselves in front of our medical captors, or scrambling to get our affairs in order, while in the prime of our life.

Look, there are no guarantees, that even if you did everything right and saved a nice nest egg, that some world event or bad investment did not change all that in an instant. We saw that with Bernie Madoff, the mastermind behind one of the largest Ponzi schemes in recent history, and later Sam Bankman Fried, the crypto tycoon who stole 10 billion dollars from his investors and was sentenced to 25 years in prison. Then, for the first time in history, your governor was able to shut down the entire state for years on end because of a rebranded flu and turn your 20-year-old conference business to dust.

Who can plan for something like that?

Similarly, we can do everything right, and have lightning strike our head when we're out for a healthy jog, or choke on a piece of grass-fed beef and suffocate on the recently mopped tile floor of your favorite steak house. But despite that, I don't think we should throw our hands up and leave the most important aspect of our life to chance. No, your health and longevity is a science worth pursuing proactively, with someone knowledgeable and trustworthy to be the fiduciary of this, your most valuable possession.

Another words, your healthspan and lifespan is a great investment and priceless legacy.

~

FINAL THOUGHT

"Most people do not really want freedom, because freedom involves responsibility, and most people are frightened of responsibility." – Sigmund Freud

Chapter 4

FREE LUNCH TRAP

Even if you got something for nothing, you got
nothing, and gave up everything.

The driver of the blue minivan only spoke a few words of English and
with a heavy Italian accent. He pulled up as I was putting quarters into a
parking meter and was about to go into a nearby office for a meeting. The
sharply dressed young man rolled down the passenger window, leaned
toward it, and asked me for directions to Kennedy Airport. We were on
Queens Boulevard in Forest Hills, so I did my best explaining how to get
to the Van Wyck Expressway from where we were standing, taking his
unfamiliarity with the language, and area, into consideration.

Grazie! he said enthusiastically. And just as he began pulling away, cobbling
together a few English words, he explained that he was coming from a
fashion show in Manhattan, and was on his way to catch a flight back
to Milan. Also, there were some leftover Armani leather jackets that he
did not want to schlep back and offered to give them to me ... at a very
nominal price.

Now, I grew up in the Soviet Union till I was ten and have experienced my
share of shysters there. Once I even had my shoes stolen as I was walking
to elementary school, in the middle of winter, while wearing them. By a
young scam artist who was a year or two my senior. I also lived and worked
in New York City for the many years since and have been on the losing

Pioneer

end of a few very slick operators. One, who reminded of Huggy Bear, from the Starsky and Hutch show, sold me a set of used bricks in a cellophane sealed box with VCR printed on the front. Then there was a woman who called my office in the shop when I was working in the West Village. She said that she's a customer and was at St. Vinsent's hospital and needed to "borrow" twenty-five dollars for her and her newborn. I looked her name up on my computer but there was nothing. When her 'friend' showed up to pick up the cash, by the looks of her, I knew that I was had. But I gave her the money anyway, 'cause you know, I promised, and I liked the chutzpah.

So, I am not someone you would call inexperienced, or credulous by any means. But he got me. I bought two jackets, with Armani, stamped all over the inside lining. It was only when I got them home and saw those jackets without all the excitement or "azart" of a deal too good to be true clouding my vision, that it dawned on me, I was bamboozled. But that was just a few hundred dollars and for what I consider a valuable life lesson. It's much worse when a sham costs us the quality of our life and ability to enjoy those things that truly matter.

Take for example the popular legerdemain that convinces us to pay $14,000 to $40,000 dollars per year for something that is misrepresented as 'health' insurance. For that money you get an annual physical ($250 value) that does NOT look for deficiencies, toxicity, or compromised system of digestion that could perhaps help you avoid illness entirely, but instead identifies early stages of disease models that can be managed for the duration of your life. With pills, band aids, defibrillators, and ambulance rides. It's kind of like bringing your car in for service. But instead of topping off the engine oil, filling up the gas tank, replacing worn brake pads, or a clogged air filter, they tell you to come back when you actually break down, and there's something more serious to fix.

So now, instead of offering a simple solution to a complicated problem, the system is actually complicit in creating the infrastructure for the delivery of complicated solutions to simple problems. Because it does not take much to add some engine oil when it's low, that's easy, inexpensive, and virtually anyone can do it. It becomes much more complicated, however, when pieces of your engine are lying on the highway and you, along with everyone you love, are stuck on the side of the road relying on the kindness of strangers to get you out of this depressing and unnerving predicament.

And it's not about prevention or early detection, it's about living life at the very peak level of health expression, right now in the moment. Making sure that your body has all the nutrients necessary for optimal function. That there is nothing interfering with the biochemical process, like heavy metal toxicity, a silent tooth infection, depleted hormones, a damaged gut lining, xenoestrogens, or parasites.

So, most people function at 50-75% capacity, thinking that their brain fog, poor sleep, inexplicable weight gain, chronic pain, fatigue, emotional instability, cognitive decline, and skin problems are just a natural part of the aging process, when nothing could be further from the truth.

YOU'RE NOT GETTING OLD YOU'RE GETTING PLAYED

The third party-payer bureaucracy has inadvertently created a system where disease, and not health, became the most profitable commodity, and the most likely outcome. So, if you happen to be looking for the permanent resolution of your chronic illness, you will never find it in a system that profits from its existence.

If there is any possibility for a cure, any hope for permanent recovery, you must work with a caring professional trained in human optimization and then develop a direct client-doctor relationship. That means you will have to scrape off the layers of bureaucracy between you and them and pay your practitioner cash on the barrel. Like you would when hiring a good attorney who needs a retainer to take on your case. Or a trusted auto-mechanic who will take the time to make sure your engine oil is topped off, the tires are safe, and your gas tank full.

Sure, some conditions are so far along, and the body defense systems so depleted, that recovery is unlikely in any system operating within the realm of reality. But for a large percentage of the population that is simply not the case. In many instances, the chronic condition can be permanently resolved when that is the actual goal. Especially, when you're working with a healer, who has made it their life mission to get to the root cause of a life-altering condition. Once you recover, and you must make yourself believe that this is a possibility, you have to engage this doctor for the duration of your life. This way for a few hundred bucks a year you can work together with your practitioner to learn the unique demands of your chemistry and genetics. So that we can keep you optimized and circumvent the many lifestyle diseases that we've come to accept as inevitable, and incurable.

By now you may be saying, sure, I can clearly see that there are two distinct systems of health care delivery. One is sponsored by layers of third party-payer bureaucracy, and waits for a disease state to manifest, so that it can be managed for the duration of my life. And the second, looks to optimize the body so that it has a fighting chance to dissipate the problem at the root. With a welcome side-effect of function at the very peak level of health expression, ageless beauty, and youthful longevity.

How then, you may be wondering, can I discern between the two systems?

Fortunately, that's simple.

Just ask if they accept your 'health' insurance.

FAIR TRADE

Perhaps you've come to a different conclusion in your life-experience, but every time I've tried to cut a corner, or get in on the cheap, it has always backfired and cost me more. Sometimes much more. Thats why, as the saying goes, mice die in traps because they don't understand why the cheese is free. So, I find it particularly confusing why so many otherwise intelligent people embrace the idea that they can have unlimited access to the time and services of highly trained professionals. Basically, saddle and harness those extraordinary people, who spent a decade of their life and a million dollars becoming doctors, like a recently purchased work horse.

So that our entitled class can fantasize about limitless care and executive treatment for free, just because they were nice enough to have been born.

What other industry allows us to think this way?

Even if all 'civilized' nations around the world have on some level implemented this fallacy, and firmly embraced this nebulous mirage of free medical care for all, that does not give it any more credence or credibility in real-world application.

Back in the day when I ran an auto repair shop in the West Village of Manhattan, I began working with a barter service. At 19 years old, I was as inexperienced as I was hungry to get my fledging business off the ground. So, when a very attractive representative of this unusual concept walked into my office and explained the system, I perked up. Basically, when someone from this group of local businesses would come to me for repairs, I would receive a check with funds that could only be used as credit within this network. She showed me a list of participating companies, which included restaurants, doctors, hairdressers, and even tailors, to name a few.

The idea was that I could use my free time to provide services to this group in exchange for any excess inventory their many members may be willing to part with. So, this system theoretically brings in clients that you would not otherwise have, while providing access to products and services that you may want, but without any out-of-pocket expense.

Sounds very reasonable and practical.

Fortunately, this barter company was happy to have me as I was the only repair shop in their well-established network. So, my team of mechanics and I became quite busy taking care of the personal vehicles of other barter members, and sometimes those that they used for their business. So, I built up a bunch of credits and decided I wanted to spend some.

The first person I went to see was a tailor, as I had a formal event coming up, and ordered two bespoke suits, to be paid for with a barter check. Long story short, after going for measurements, corrections, and adjustments numerous times, in frustration I ended up throwing both suits away. Turns out he repurposed them from some extremely large athlete-type and simply made the sleeves and pants shorter. At first, I couldn't understand why when I lifted my arms the sleeves would slide up to my elbows. It took me a moment to figure out that instead of throwing those suits in the incinerator like he should have, after Shrek neglected to pick them up, he decided to unload them in exchange for some barter bucks.

Then I took my wife and two-year-old son for a photo shoot at a studio that was pretty pricey, but since it was not really money but barter, I was happy to do it. We spent about an hour there, and this photographer took some really great shots, I know, because the one she gave me I still have framed on my wall. But then she called and said that she could not afford to do this deal through barter, and if I wanted the rest of the pictures, I would need to pay her a significant portion of the cost in cash.

Another time I took my team out for dinner to a restaurant that was in my barter network. There were about 12 of us who enjoyed the unimpressive food and lackluster ambiance of this otherwise empty and out of the way bistro. Finally, as I was filling out a barter check, the manager informed me unapologetically that they don't know what that is, and since the owner was not there, I had to pay cash.

The last example I'll share here is the dentist I went to because I was experiencing extreme sensitivity to hot and cold. After multiple visits, he finished filing two of my teeth to the knub and drilling some of the others, when he finally discovered the cavity in an entirely different tooth that was so obvious, even I could see it, when he showed it to me on the x-ray. Now many years since I'm still dealing with the residual ramifications of the clumsy efforts of this senior citizen who was a few clicks past his expiration date.

So, in my experience, even though barter is a nice idea, I found that it did not work in practice as well as it sounded in theory.

The idea with 'health' insurance, like that of a gym membership, is that hopefully you'll be one of the many paying members who never bothers to use it. With most of that relationship consisting of you delivering exorbitant monthly payments to their plush office. I have a friend who joined virtually every gym in our area and was a faithful member for many years, although he almost never went. Once he called me up and told me about a great deal offered by a local gym and asked if I wanted to go with him to check it out. We both ended up joining, but that first day was his one and only time there, for the rest of his annual commitment. And as strange as that may sound, it's not at all uncommon. Because depending on who you listen to, anywhere from 20 -70% of all memberships go completely unused. So, a gym can sell 10,000 memberships even though their capacity is only 3,000 or so.

All the above systems are just concepts, someone's ideas that have been introduced to the market in the hope of making things better for the public, and perhaps turning into a profitable endeavor for the proprietor. Usually, these nice sounding ideas are embraced by a new generation of people who no longer give much thought to how they've come to be, and if in this current environment this approach is still the most viable, and practical option.

Each of these paradigms are driven by the philosophy of its architect, and may even seem plausible on the surface, yet become problematic in practice every time and everywhere they are tried. Both socialism and capitalism are such ideas. The former promises equity, and fairness, as a small group of selfless elites' control and plan the economy from the top down. Attempting to orchestrate millions of interactions between little understood desires, preferences, resources, and needs of the unique individual, so that ostensibly greed and profit are removed from the equation. And honestly, if I had never heard of socialism, and did not live within the crumbling walls of this soul sucking gulag, I think I could have been easily sold on the idea.

As the sales pitch goes: we're all going to live together in unity, helping one another, and then each of us will get what we need, and produce what we are able. Or in the much more eloquent words of Karl Marx "From each according to his ability, to each according to his needs." We will remove jealousy from society, as everyone will have access to everything they require, and it will be more affordable and less expensive since we eradicate all the middlemen between the citizen and the state. But of course, eventually it turns into: *you will have nothing, eat bugs, and be happy.*

Sign me up!

Unfortunately, however, the darn reality gets in the way every time. No matter how you try you will never be able to change human nature. You can subjugate it, murder it by the millions, you can starve it to death, and imprison it under inhumane conditions. You can brainwash it with daily propaganda, torture, and institutionalize it, but you will never be able to change it at the fundamental core.

Kind of like the wind.

You can spend your entire life and effort wrestling with it and screaming at it, or you can just set your sails correctly, and work with reality as it comes, to achieve the desired outcome. Human nature as well can be worked with, and when treated with the respect it deserves, it responds accordingly. Like a flower that opens its petals after the sun provided it with enough warmth and attention. Similarly, the right environment of freedom, inspiration, and limitless opportunity can naturally bring out the best in people.

In this unique context, one guided by the invisible hand operating within the confines of a free society, we can become more kind, generous, and thoughtful. We enthusiastically pursue the cultivation of creativity, courage, patience, and love. We will even volunteer to risk and sacrifice our life, if need be, for the things we believe to be right and good. We will spend half of our life working hard serving humanity, accumulating astronomical wealth, and then spend the other half of our life working just as hard, giving it all away to causes we consider important.

Remarkable philanthropic works that serve the greater good, like building libraries, hospitals, and colleges across the nation, feeding the hungry, or preserving art and history for future generations. In fact, the citizens of the Unites States donate a half trillion dollars per year to worthy causes.

Making it the most generous nation by far.

The best system that has ever been tried to achieve those things, and cultivate the most beautiful innate nature of mankind, has been capitalism, within a constitutional democracy. One would think that this fact should be self-evident as it birthed the greatest nation in the history of man. Not perfect or utopian, but great in just about every respect. Sadly, way too many people who were born here do not appreciate the level of remarkability that should be assigned to this experiment in economics, human behavior, hierarchy, and evolution. Perhaps as a fish can have no concept of being out of water, unless one day it finds itself wildly flapping and gasping for life on some lonely pier, it will never develop the healthy respect for the life-giving power that being in water makes possible.

When the Soviet Union was alive and well, the people living in the United States had something to compare capitalism to. And most intelligent people saw that the free market and its invisible hand was a much better philosophical system to live under than communism and its iron fist. So, if you wanted to be independent, say whatever you thought true without fear of retaliation or imprisonment, live wherever you wanted, practice your religion, eat regularly, sleep soundly, and accumulate as much wealth that your talents, education, and work ethic permit; it was a no brainer.

If you ever read 'Witness' by Whittaker Chambers, this real-life spy drama documents the underworld of the communist movement in the United States during the 1930's by a man who drank the tainted cool-aid and lived to talk about it. He worked with top US officials, corrupted by this evil idea, and the empire that embraced and promulgated it. Eventually, this writer and intellectual was able to see how callous and brutal this dead-end Soviet philosophy was. Testifying in front of congress and exposing the perpetrators in minute detail throughout the amazing story played out in 718 pages of his bestselling and thrilling book.

This author's passionate testimony and meticulous documentation, resulted in the criminal indictment of Alger Hiss, a State Department official and one of the leaders of this dark cabal within the echelon of the US government.

HAVE YOU CONSIDERED DYING

A couple of years after I became interested in the topic, of this curiosity, that is our system of indefinite management of chronic disease (IMCD) industrial complex, I invited the president of Physicians for a National Health Program (PNHP) for a radio interview. This group was founded in 1988 and represents some 25,000 doctor-members throughout the United States. At the time I was very green and a little more than intimidated by this confident, experienced, and otherwise brilliant man. During our conversation, he referenced the Canadian system of health care as a model that we should try to emulate here in the United States. Where the government provided healthcare to their population at absolutely no cost. Known as the 'one-payer' option where all the services were priced and reimbursed by the federal government of Canada. Citizens of course paid higher taxes, but it was a small price, he assured me, to have what is ultimately free and limitless access to first world care anytime you need it.

He led me around like a puppy with his, "one-payer is not socialized medicine", "the doctors will still maintain autonomy" and "health care is a human right." Then he went for the kill with: "You'll have unlimited access and better care, even though all the payments will come from the government, saving the overhead, and removing the profit margins inherent to a free-market business like that of an insurance company."

And although he was very convincing, I was not very convinced.

Some years later, I interviewed a doctor from Canada, who founded the first privately owned MRI center in Quebec and was offering this service to people before it was legal to do so. And for cash. As it turned out, when the Canadian government inevitably started running out of other people's money, they began rationing access to important screening services, where you would need to wait more than six months to get an MRI scan. Forcing some creative people to make an appointment with a local veterinarian, pay cash, and get the scan virtually immediately, albeit on all fours.

Today, it's becoming very clear, to those of us who have their eyes even slightly open, that this particular national health program resulted in the inevitable implementation of the Medical Assistance in Dying (MAID) initiative. Now that Eutopia Medical of Canada ran out of money, it's not able to tax people any more without inciting a revolution or permit the queue to become any more ridiculously long. The only logical next step is to invite terminal, difficult, and expensive patients to consider a medical procedure that will end their life. Since (MAID) became legal in 2016, doctor assisted euthanasia quickly became the third biggest killer of Canadians.

There is a popular meme that highlights this phenomenon. Where England offers a solution for the "I need stitches" problem with 'you'll have to wait 43 months', in the United States, 'it will cost you $67,000', and in Canada, 'have you considered dying?'

Perhaps P.J. O'Rourke, the American Journalist and author, was not just talking about money when he said, "if you think healthcare is expensive now just wait until it's free."

WITH AN IRON FIST

The one thing about the Soviet Union that was good, for the leaders of the Soviet Union, is that they did not permit dissenting opinions or offered a platform for competing ideas. As Ronald Reagan famously told the humorous story he shared with Mikhail Gorbachev, (the last leader of the Soviet Union before Perestroika) about an American and a Russian arguing about who was living under the better system. The American said, our system is so free and good, that I can walk into the oval office slam my fist on the President's desk, look him in the eye, and say, Mr. President, I don't like how you're running this country. Ha, the Russian answered, I can do dat. I can valk into the Kremlin, bang my fist on the General Secretary's desk, look him in the eye, and tell him, Mr. Secretary I don't like how President Reagan is running his country.

That's funny because no one can tell Vladimir Putin or his predecessors how to run Russia. And if you bang your fist on his proverbial desk, you will lose the proverbial fist, and perhaps more likely, your life. Some of the oligarchs have tried to challenge his inexorable rule and ended up paying a tremendous price. Mikhail Khodorkovsky was at the top of the Forbes list of the wealthiest people in the world. A very smart, tough, and ambitious man I imagine. After taking over some of the Siberian oil fields, when perestroika unraveled the Soviet Union in the early 1990's, he built the Yukos Oil Company to eventually produce 20% or Russia's energy output. By 2003 he was considered the wealthiest man in Russia with a reported fortune of 16 billion dollars.

When he challenged Putin, the former KGB foreign intelligence officer however, in a run for the presidency of the Russian Federation, he simultaneously challenged his well-entrenched ideas and dogma. This was a fierce battle of wealth, power, political savvy, and vision for the future of Russia post the collapse of the Soviet experiment. In 2003 Mikhail was arrested by the authorities, who charged him with fraud, taking the wind out of his political sails. Then, his assets were seized, and Mikhail was sentenced to 9 years, later extended to 13 years, in "Matrosskaya Tishina" prison in Moscow.

Which literally translates into "Sailors Silence".

So, let that be a lesson, to all would be challengers of the dictatorial powers of the freely elected president. Of what is clearly no longer a totalitarian empire. Perhaps Mikhail should thank his lucky stars as he was eventually released after serving only 10 years in a Russian prison. Because more recently Alexi Navalny, the 46-year-old leader of the opposition party, and staunch critic of this regime, was not so fortunate.

Here in the United States, with the freedom of speech that the First Amendment chiseled into the US Constitution in 1791, we are asked to exercise restraint as we watch the vilest kind of philosophies and ideas cast stones at our beautiful and patient Democratic Republic paradigm. Repeatedly turning the other cheek, in the hope that this fragile idea, build by imperfect but honorable men, is impervious to the onslaught, and can withstand these ongoing assaults.

In fact, perhaps becoming stronger because of them.

So, we put up with an angry priest yelling at his congregants to GD damn America. Allowing Nazis to rally on our streets. Permitting the Communist Party USA to exist and host a website. Have the Democratic Socialists of America solicit donations, and now entertain multiple groups with a rainbow of sexual preferences and insatiable demands. Men in skirts and hair ribbons who fight women in the octagon, crossdressers in teased wigs who teach twerking to children, and the outspoken BLM Marxists who spent an entire summer libeling everyone racist, while lighting our cities on fire, in the name of freedom of expression, and justice for all.

Here's how this idea is worded:

"Congress shall make no law respecting an establishment of religion or prohibiting the free exercise thereof; or abridging the freedom of speech, or of the press; or the right of the people peaceably to assemble, and to petition the Government for a redress of grievances."

Certainly, how can one disagree with something so wholesome and empowering. Although when I see people burn the American Flag, set buildings on fire during mostly peaceful protests, loot businesses with impunity, tear down our history, and shout "death to America". I feel like this is a great place to draw the line and banish our domestic enemies to a communist or Islamist country for at least a year. It can be turned into a reality show, we'll call it "Snowflakes in the Desert". The profits from which can be used to offset the cost for their economy flight, and complementary, full body hijab with eye veil.

But this is probably the soviet child in me speaking.

BLOOD DIAMONDS

When you add a relatively harmless mentos to an innocuous bottle of carbonated soda, the reaction is dangerously explosive, as I'm sure you've seen in some of the videos posted online. Similarly, both capitalism and socialism are for the most part cordial when kept in their separate corners. Although socialism, like soda, has been known to rot your teeth, destroy your wellbeing, and ravage the gut biome permitting a candida infestation that makes life unbearable.

Sort of speak.

Still, it's not nearly as bad when the two are combined. Perhaps modern China is a good example. For a long time, they practiced their form of communism. They ate rice. They lived in fear. They starved and died by the millions. They were herded into re-education camps in matching outfits. And prostrated themselves in front of portraits and statues of their comrade leaders.

It was the normal outcome of this evil ideology.

But when they permitted independent people to run their own businesses. Buy and cultivate land and live what we would call a more freedom-based, entrepreneurial lifestyle, that's when things started getting hairy. Now the economy began to grow exponentially, the population became wealthier, and the country jumped as a large player onto the world stage. Except the government still controls the business and the people, managing the economy and the masses with an iron fist. So, technically, when you combine socialism and capitalism, what inevitably blows out of the bottle's neck is some new version of fascism.

I know this sounds a bit dramatic. But hear me out. Our health care system was pretty simple at one point and not so long ago. People who could afford it paid the doctor directly or bought health insurance, so that if they were in an accident or got sick unexpectedly, they could go to the doctor and all of the expenses were paid by a community that pooled a small portion of their wages. Those who did not have the money usually relied on a very robust charity network that helped people access the care they needed. It was a community based, people helping people, kind of environment. And maybe it was not perfect, I'm sure some people were not able to get the kind of care they wanted, and many had to do without. So, at some point we decided to mix the business of health care with the mighty bureaucracy of the government, and what blew out of the bottle neck is this one-eyed cyclops with a bad attitude and insatiable appetite.

When on July 30th, 1965, Lyndon B. Johnson signed the Medicare and Medicaid Act into law, and as that mentos hit the soda water with a splash the whole thing began to percolate. And from that moment on, our health care expense, along with the obesity epidemic, and all the related co-morbidities began to grow exponentially.

From a relatively small 27 billion dollars per year budget in the early 1960's the health care expense hit a trillion dollars in 1995. The question that is being begged here, is what came first, the chicken, or this ridiculously convoluted omelet, with a mountain of broken eggs needed to make it. Did we all of a sudden become so sickly as a society, as US citizens, and as human beings, that we needed a trillion dollars' worth of medical intervention? Or is it because we started dumping all of this money into the indefinite management of chronic disease, inadvertently turning chronic disease into a very profitable and therefore desirable commodity?

Well, to answer this question.

What never happened in the history of mankind, and we did in a very short 30 years, we repeated in the following ten. Because from 1995 to 2005 the health care system doubled to two trillion dollars. And one would have to assume that our health as a nation became twice as bad.

At this point if anyone has any doubt that our sickness and disease has been turned into some version of a blood diamond, from 2005 to today the healthcare system doubled again and as of 2022 we're spending 4.5 trillion dollars every year, quickly heading to 5 trillion. And only two possible things can come out of this lamentable trajectory, either we're going to run out of paper necessary to print the money to pay for this bureaucracy, or we're going to run out of people healthy enough to get out of bed in the morning.

Fortunately, we in the United States lead the world in health and longevity. Unfortunately, it's the third world. So, we live 15 minutes longer than people in Uganda, North Korea, Iran, Pakistan, Somalia. Of course, we're spending $13,493 dollars per capita, to achieve these very impressive outcomes, while it cost them like seven seashells and a chicken. People in the civilized world on the other hand, Japan for example, live into their late 80's or 90's and then they die, and sometimes while executing a difficult move on the dance floor.

Or the bedroom.

What we've inadvertently done is mix the proverbial menthols that is 'we the people' with the carbonated soda that is 'they the government'. So today we have 'everybody' that is the 330 or so million US citizens, who placed 'everybody' that is the almost three million federal government employees, in charge of our system of healthcare. Therefore, it is these people who we don't know and have never met that today preside over our health, life, happiness, and freedom.

And I believe we're intelligent enough to understand that when you have 'everybody' responsible for 'everybody', technically, you have nobody responsible for anyone.

~

FINAL THOUGHT

"Medicine is the keystone of the arch of
socialism." – Vladimir Ilyich Lenin

Chapter 5

THE CROWNING DECADE

The most valuable commodity in the world is the
one that has been virtually depleted.

When I was a boy growing up in Soviet Russia, my father was important enough in the entrepreneur underground, or the black market within the shadows of the socialist paradise, if you prefer. To be able to buy Beluga Caviar in a five pound can on a somewhat regular basis. It was blue and round, the size of a small hat box, with a thick orange rubber band around the middle of the tin can where the cover connected to the base. Once open it looked like a million tiny glistening, black pearls that smelled of salt and sea, and opulence. Of course, in contrast, my little brother, my mother, dad, dog and I, lived in a tiny one-bedroom apartment on the fourth floor of a decrepit government-owned walk up.

At a recent art show in Manhattan's SOHO neighborhood that we attended, they were serving Champagne, and black caviar. But out of a can the size of a thimble, placing just a few grains on a tiny cracker perfect for a tea party hosted by Thumbelina. I smiled at the memory of me sinking a tablespoon into that freshly opened ocean of fish eggs, as if it were a bottomless bowl of cornflakes.

Over the last 100 or so years the world developed a taste for this delicacy resulting in overfishing of the Sturgeon in the Black and Caspian Sea, causing inevitable shortages, high demand, and exorbitant prices that

Yury

reached critical levels in recent years. Threatening this, the largest freshwater fish in the world, with extinction. Fortunately, however, even at $35,000 per kg., you can still get yourself as much of these fancy fish eggs as you wish, and that your personal financial resources permit. Even better, Mark Zaslavsky, founder of Sturgeon Aqua Farms in Bason, FL spent the last 20 years growing sturgeons to maturity in giant water tanks. As the only such producer in the US, he says that in a few years, there will be plenty of caviar to go around and perhaps more affordably and sustainably than ever before.

He even has a plan to replenish the Sturgeon population in the Caspian Sea, which is remarkable. That's the great thing about the free market, as it creates more of the things it knows it will profit from and that the world demands. That's why I don't think we will ever run out of chicken, lamb, or cattle. On the other hand, the socialists, those self-appointed arbiters of environmental causes, fished the Sturgeon to oblivion as fast as possible, giving little thought to its probable and eternal disappearance.

But that's what happens in desperation and scarcity. In the iconic book Gulag Archipelago, Alexander Solzhenitsyn, who spent eight years in one of the most brutal prisons of the Soviet Union, shares a story of how some of the prisoners in the frozen tundra of a Siberian labor camp, found a prehistoric fauna that was probably 10,000 years old.

Here, we who live in the abundance of the first world, would probably call archeologists and explore the origins, history, and meaning of this fish or lizard, or dinosaur. But of course, there, they hastily broke the ice, dragged their trophy close to the open fire so it could thaw, and ate it.

I HAD A BEAUTIFUL DREAM

The law of scarcity that applies to our lifespan, however, is not the same. As we get into the final decade of our time on this planet each moment becomes more precious than the last. And all the money in the world won't buy you an extra minute of this priceless and finite resource. There is just no way to find and defrost more time I'm afraid. Of course, for the most part, we have no idea when that final decade will be. Barring any accident or violence, it's hard to tell how long our bodies will last, and plan accordingly. Will we make it to 78, which is the average lifespan for men in the United States or get closer to the other side of statistical possibilities and live to be 90. Perhaps a few of us will be so fortunate as to live to 100 or beyond and join that exclusive centenarian club.

But much more important than how long we live; is how long we live well. Till what point of our life are we able to lift our grandchildren high above our head, drive our cars, travel the world, belly laugh, and experience the people we love as we did in our younger years. Those sunny years that we took mostly for granted and consumed the days with a tablespoon as if it was a bottomless bowl of proverbial cornflakes. Perhaps it has never been more obvious as our political leaders enter their eighties and are showing significant signs of rapid decline. We of course accept this as the reality of our world. We see it all around us, and in our mind, we start believing that this is our inevitable fate as well. Usually either dismissing this reality to be of any significance, fall into a terror spiral, or ignore it completely, trying to distract ourselves from the frightening powerlessness we have in the face of our own mortality.

My belief, one I cultivate and pursue daily, is that living till 100 vibrant, productive, and fulfilling years is my birthright, and mandate. How this belief manifests itself in reality matters little, but the way it gets me to behave in the moment is crucial.

Because 'old' is psychology not chronology.

Although my family history is not abundant with the long-lived and is permeated with all kinds of health issues. Ones that took the life of some of the people I love much too early. Perhaps leaving decades of good living on the proverbial table. My maternal grandfather, Boris, who fought the fascists during the war, for example, developed diabetes later in life resulting in the amputation of his right leg just below the knee, leaving him with limited mobility for some 5 years before he eventually passed at 86. On my dad's side, my father is the youngest of four children, his brother who was 13 years his senior and obese for most of his adult life, died from heart disease at a young 73. We lost his oldest sister to lung cancer at just 59, and the other one has been living with a debilitating autoimmune condition virtually her entire life.

Recently we lost my younger brother to colon cancer, which to me, is the most tragic.

It came as a shock, primarily because it was less than a year from diagnosis to funeral. He moved his family to a small town in Pennsylvania over a decade before, some 3-4 hours from the area of Long Island where he lived just a few minutes away from me. So, we did not see each other very often, and I really had no idea how bad things were until it became blatantly obvious. He was so optimistic and dismissive about the entire thing that the times we spoke it never entered my mind that he would not recover. When my mom mentioned that the doctors told him to plan for 'end of life', I found myself hyperventilating.

It was a lovely funeral, on a freezing and windy day towards the end of February, at a small cemetery in Easton Pennsylvania just a couple of weeks after his fiftieth birthday. My mom with her new husband, and my dad who flew in from Moscow alone, as well as dozens of our cousins and scores of his friends attended. Witnessing the heartbreak of the moment I walked solemnly through memory lane as I looked at the gallery of photos displayed of my little brother living his life. One was a portrait of him from first grade, where he was wearing his blue uniform jacket, a white collared shirt, and that red five-star pin with a childhood portrait of Lenin in the center, on his lapel. Offering condolences, while embracing his wife of 25 years, and their three grown children as they stood guard next to the open casket, tore at my soul, and aged me like nothing else I've experienced till this moment.

What is the most perplexing and infuriating perhaps, is that I've learned from my ScHO physicians many years ago, and as I already mentioned, there is a direct correlation between vitamin D deficiency and cancer. With a 75% chance of developing colon cancer when your levels of this crucial pre-hormone are below 20 ng/mL (nanograms per milliliter) for an extended period. When I tried to find out his levels no one seemed interested enough to tell me. So, after months of surgery that he referred to with a smirk, as 'them going medieval'. He passed quietly with my mom and his wife standing over him and sobbing while holding each of his hands, as he lay on a mechanized bed in a sterile and well-lit room of a Manhattan cancer hospital.

Honestly, there was probably not much anyone would be able to do for him as the diagnosis came so late and the cancer metastasized to other organs, a full year before a colonoscopy was historically recommended. Of course, now they suggest you get your first test at 45, as so many more young people are being lost to this modern scourge. Sadly, instead of trying to understand why this tragedy is trickling down to people in the prime of their life, we are simply expanding the scope of testing and early diagnosis. It's like developing multiple leaks in your roof, and then running around the house placing buckets under them so the water won't damage your parquet floor. Instead of going up and scraping off all the shingles, finding the rotten wood and replacing it.

So, as we were designing this Science of Human Optimization model, I had my brother, and this paradox, at the forefront of my thinking. What if someone sold him on a more proactive approach to care a decade or two before his diagnosis? What if over that time we raised and kept his vitamin D level between 80-100 ng/mL as I prefer mine be. What if we tested his digestive biome and discovered the depletion of important bugs like Akkermansia for example, responsible for digestion and assimilation of vital nutrients from the food he was consuming, and usually found in abundance in those people who live to be 100 and beyond?

What if we found that his food choices were lacking important vitamins, or were full of gluten saturated with glyphosate, a broad-spectrum herbicide, that was wreaking havoc with his digestive tract? What if we tested him for mold, or xenoestrogens, or heavy metals, as my friend Leigh Erin Connealy, MD author of *The Cancer Revolution: A Groundbreaking Program to Reverse and Prevent Cancer*, and one of the top functional oncologists in the country recommends to her patients, who already have cancer. In this case not because we were forced to do it but as an insurance policy of sorts. Isn't it easier to remove mold or mercury, as you optimize your vitamin D levels when you are not under the threat of a terminal diagnosis, with a rapidly approaching expiration date, and before it causes damage that may be irreversible?

Who knows, is the answer to all that.

But somewhere in my wildest fantasies this tragedy would have never happened, and he would not know anything different. Yury would just be going on the next trip to Italy with his wife whose family still has property on the countryside near Milan, complaining about the price of tickets, traffic, and her taking too long to pack.

But now that is simply a beautiful dream.

BAG OF DIAMONDS

Some 80 guests made it to the restaurant after the cemetery and were there eating and speaking in hushed, somber tones. By then I was pretty intoxicated and lightheaded although I did not drink or eat anything. I was walking around in a daze saying hello to relatives I haven't seen in years. When my wife suggested I say something, an impromptu eulogy of sorts. Getting everyone's attention was not difficult as I stood in front of the room thinking of what to say, people began looking in my direction as the place became eerily quiet, in what I would call a pregnant moment.

The first words were clumsy, spoken through a fog of mind, throat constricted, and eyes burning as if I was engulfed in a cloud of pepper spray, making it difficult to see people's reactions. It took a minute of mumbling and circling when I finally figured out what it was that I wanted to say.

There was this young couple, I began, who were very poor. They were walking through Central Park holding hands and talking about their future together. As they sat on a bench overlooking a pond, he handed her a small bag of peanuts, and on the side, it said, "I wish this bag of peanuts was a bag of diamonds".

Well, many years later they became wealthy and successful, and eventually as the top of the hourglass ran out of those precious grains of time, he found himself on his deathbed, with her holding his hand they were reminiscing about their life together. This time he handed her a bag of diamonds, and on the side, it said, "I wish this bag of diamonds was a bag of peanuts".

This was the story that the priest who presided at my brother's wedding shared all those years ago and I thought it was appropriate for the moment. As everyone who loved my brother yearned for the days when he made us laugh uproariously, hosted dinners for all our cousins, dismissed all worldly problems in his upbeat and optimistic manner, and made life so much more interesting and fun for everyone who knew him.

There we all were, holding the proverbial bag of diamonds, eager to trade it for a bag of peanuts.

GOOD GENETICS

One of my earliest memories of my paternal grandmother was her sitting in a small wooden kiosk, a much simpler version of the ones you see in Manhattan today that sell candy, gum, newspapers, and magazines. In Russia it was Pravda (truth) that was the main publication disseminating daily propaganda to the passing crowds on their way to government jobs. She worked a couple of blocks away from the building where she lived with one of her adult daughters, and her daughter's toddler. This was the middle of a cold Moscow winter famous for crushing its enemies. It was also pretty harsh on those who lived there, and who it may have considered friends. She just sat there most of the day selling filtered truth and unfiltered cigarettes. No window, bathroom, or heat, with a wool scarf (some call 'babushka' a word that literally translates into grandmother) covering her head, and fingerless gloves so that she could handle money and merchandise.

Her husband Leonid, my father's dad, also fought the nazis during the war, and when he came home in May of 1945, he had to fight the soviets for his family's survival. Working at a food processing plant, he could not take any extra meat to feed his children, because there was no extra. But he was able to get his hands on a cowhide in a backroom deal, that he exchanged for some extra milk and bread. He received 10 years for 'subversive activities' and was sent to a brutal gulag. When he finally came back, he was very sick and died shortly thereafter. With my dad, who was ten years old by then, holding the hand of a man he only met a couple of times.

EVOLUTION BY DESIGN

Grandma Zina was born in May of 1914, in Berdichev, which was the fourth largest city in Ukraine, and predominantly Jewish. After her husband's death in 1956 she never remarried and remained dedicated to her children and later grandchildren exclusively. I remember visiting her often, and two things stand out, she made the most delicious cookies when I was a child. And at times invited me for a shot of Cognac when I became an adult, as she was convinced this golden elixir dilated the vessels and improved blood flow.

She was also about 50-80 pounds overweight, during all the years I knew her, and ate a diet mostly procured from the local Russian store, with kielbasa, pelmeni (meat dumplings), bread, and sweets as staples. To her credit she did walk regularly for exercise, later using a cane, not because she needed it, but because she wanted to ward off the evil eye, as was her explanation. Even though she was not what one would call health-conscious, my grandma lived to be an impressive 96, mostly vibrant and independent years.

Like many people of that time, she was not so much interested in health or longevity, but survival. How do we find enough food to feed the children who are hungry? How do we avoid the fascists from executing our family as they did so many others? How do we stay clear of being sent to the gulag and at the same time procure firewood to heat the house? How do we survive the pogroms and Stalin's diabolical plan to eradicate the Jews and the intellectuals? How do we escape to a country where we can live in freedom, peace, and perhaps even prosperity?

Well, times have changed, and many of the things that concerned my grandparents and parents are not even on the radar of my children. That is a blessing for sure. Our priorities have changed, and our goals and aspirations, should probably keep up. Today's scientific and technological advances are truly hard to comprehend for us and were unimaginable for them. People from a time of no indoor plumbing who had to walk to town to use a telephone. From our ubiquitous smart phones to powerful computers, Chat GPT, our growing understanding of genetics, digestive biome research, blood chemistry analysis using artificial intelligence (AI), and CRISPR-Cas9 the breakthrough science that can edit the genetics of an individual, and literally cut out the genes that cause a particular disease.

So why would we only want to use this science and technology reactively, and not use it for human optimization as it were? Does it make any sense to first develop an avoidable and deadly condition and then scramble to learn about all the remarkable advances that can perhaps ameliorate the symptoms? When alternatively, we could have used it all along to not only avoid this tsunami of modern illnesses but get as much life-energy available, in the deep reserves of its limitless potential. Animating this remarkable lump of clay that each of us received, to navigate and experience this world thoroughly, and for as long as possible.

Imagine for a moment if we start with my grandmother Zina's, great, great, granddaughter and do things completely differently. She is just a year old as of this writing. Very cute I should add. What if we did her genetics now and made a plan of what kind of nutrition, lifestyle, and fitness habits we can help her learn as she is figuring out the nuances of speaking, eating, and walking independently? How long can we get her to live and how many of the modern health issues can we help her avoid if we approach this scientifically, proactively, and immediately.

Can we save her the pain of trying all the different diets to constantly wrestle with her weight or heal her acne, or deal with ADHD, anxiety, and depression as a young adult? While living under the genetic threat of diabetes, obesity, heart disease, cancer, and autoimmune problems? Certainly, the smarter thing to do would be to provide her with all the necessary resources, and building blocks for growing tall, strong, and beautiful, with silky hair, bright eyes and a clear sharp mind.

Isn't this what human evolution is all about?

WE CARE SO VERY MUCH

How would you want to spend your final decade on this earth if you had anything to say about it? Like me, I'm sure you don't want to be in a lovely retirement home, sitting in a sunlit corner and drooling in your soup under someone's supervision. That, I don't think, is anyone's definition of success.

Unfortunately, this is exactly what, I believe, the matrix has planned for all of us.

One of my clients owned a powerlifting studio located in proximity to a large nursing home. She met some of the managers and staff who oversaw a large population of seniors, many of whom could no longer walk and were relegated to wheelchairs. She innocently offered to bring some training classes to this facility free of charge. Within weeks a miracle happened, as some of the people who could not walk before suddenly regained their strength and independence. And you'd think that everyone there would be very excited about the turn of events and make her services a permanent part of the offerings. But that is not the case. They politely but firmly asked her to leave and never come back. As she was threatening their business model of caring for those who could no longer care for themselves.

Now granted, this is anecdotal evidence, as I was not there when the original conversation happened and was not a witness to the events firsthand.

But this is not the first time I hear this kind of story.

Many years ago, when I was passionately into self-development and personal growth, I went to a conference on a topic that had nothing to do with health or longevity. One of the presenters, who was teaching a course on memory and visualization, shared a story that I remember clearly all these decades later. He once worked for a nursing home as a consultant and took a sample group of wilting seniors with Alzheimer's and such, through a somewhat unique protocol. He made sure they got enough sunlight, exercise, some diet modification, and basic supplements. Once again, the results were so impressive that he was summarily kicked out, so that the perverse incentives that kept that boat steady were not upset. I could see the bewilderment and hurt in his eyes as he shared the story, and the memory of the unfairness of it registered emotionally in my very being.

Neither you nor I can prove any of this of course, but if you remember the scene in the Pearl Harbor movie, when Captain Harold Thurman, the navy intelligence officer, played by Dan Aykroid explains his theory of why he believes the attack on the Pacific Fleet was imminent. "We have to interpret what we think they are trying to do" he said, "it's like playing chess in the dark, any rumor, spine tingle, goose bump we pay attention to it." Like me, he was certain of what was going to happen, because of an overwhelming amount of circumstantial evidence, but could not provide enough tangible proof in time for the leadership to take the necessary precautions.

Well, I'm sure that the last decade of life, here in the United States will be very expensive. Monetarily speaking it can cost as much as a million dollars in health-related services. Like with anything else today, it's difficult to find the exact numbers, because all the search engines are only interested in showing you what the powers that be want you to see. Sadly, there is some daylight between that and the reality we will have to endure. But regardless, if you are well, spry, and independent for that crowning decade, living life on your terms as it were, you are then not profitable to this bureaucracy in any way, and that is just not patriotic.

To achieve independence, to live a longer and healthier life, you must have a little bit of a rebellious spirit, a shtickle of chutzpah, as well as a lively sense of humor. And trust the experts, as much as you would any stranger telling you that they are here to help.

And that they care so very much.

~

FINAL THOUGHT

"Time is free, but it's priceless. You can't own it, but you can use it. You can't keep it, but you can spend it. Once you've lost it you can never get it back." - Harvey Mackay

Chapter 6

HEALTHSPAN

You will either spend all your pennies trying to stay
well or all your savings trying to get well.

When I first met Richard Linchitz, he was working out of a tiny basement office in an antiquated building in Glen Cove NY, with ash trays above the urinals, in the circa 1970's bathrooms. It was not always so for this remarkable man. Rick, as he preferred to be called, was a medical doctor directing one of the largest pain management clinics in the Northeast. He was board certified in psychiatry, neurology, pain management, and eventually, anti-aging medicine. A triathlete, author, physician, world-renowned lecturer on numerous topics, and one of the most impressive and humble men I've ever met. Two years prior to our first meeting, he was diagnosed with terminal lung cancer known as broncho-alveolar carcinoma, a rare condition that eventually took his life.

Just after his fiftieth birthday he was given only two years to live by his oncologist. And it was this prognosis that sent him around the world searching for anything that may stave off this tragic end to what was a remarkable life. To the bewilderment of his doctors, he lived another 15 amazing years, while using what he learned, to transform the lives of thousands of people like me, who were fortunate enough to find their way to his brilliant, intuitive, and cause-focused approach to what we now call, science of human optimization.

Richard Linchitz, MD

When I saw him for the very last time, about two weeks prior to his passing, I asked if there was a message he wanted to share with the world. This is what he said: *"Completely Accepting Reality as it Presents Itself is the Essence of Peace."* Don't take things personally, whatever comes your way is either an opportunity to learn, awake, or transcend. It's all good and there is richness in everything we must face if we are to live fully and discover our own power by stretching to the very edge of our potential.

This way of looking at the world made Rick an inspiration in life, and then eventually, in death.

His wife Rita, who is a nurse by training and very spiritual by nature, shared with me some years later that when she proposed the idea that perhaps the purpose of his suffering was to save his children and loved ones from a bad omen, he quietly responded: 'then bring it on'. Rick spent those precious years working as hard as ever and kept a rigorous schedule of a much younger man, one not living under the ominous threat of a terminal illness. His practice grew rapidly and within three years he was back on top of the world, literally. Now working out of a 5000 sq foot office on the highest floor of the tallest office building in the area, with 19 doctors and professionals working with him. His own schedule booked months in advance as he focused on cancer patients exclusively.

His mission was to bring true healing, and not just symptom management, to those people afflicted with cancer, and who traveled to The Linchitz Wellness center from around the world. You could say that he was a functional medicine doctor before such titles were readily offered or the concept well understood. What he was, or became, is someone who did things that made sense, and most importantly, ones that generated positive, and at times miraculous results for his patients.

OUT OF THE BOX CARE

Donato Perez Garcia is a third-generation physician who practiced in Mexico City with a focus on a particular treatment that his grandfather, a Medical Doctor born in 1893, developed many decades earlier, and that his father later helped perfect over a lifetime of practicing medicine.

It's called Insulin Potentiation Therapy (IPT).

It is well known in the medical community that cancer loves sugar, or glucose, which can come from bread and pasta, as well as cake and candy. In fact, when they use a PET scan, first a form of radioactive sugar known as radionucleotide, is administered either orally or intravenously. Which is absorbed by the cancer cell at a much higher rate than a regular cell, and then lights up in the findings providing the oncologist with a road map of sorts. What Dr. Garcia' grandfather did was to similarly administer glucose to the patient first, and then once the cancer opened its many receptors, filling up on its favorite desert, he administered a drop of chemotherapy. About 10% of the usual dose. The cancer cell would then take in some 1000 times the amount of medicine than it would otherwise.

I once had dinner with Dr. Garcia and his lovely wife. They flew to New York at our invitation, to speak at the conference we produced, in a hotel near Times Square. I picked them up from the airport and drove to a Russian restaurant in Brooklyn. There, over some borsht and lambchops, he shared the story of his legacy, the origins of this innovative therapy and its efficacy with me candidly, and in much more detail. He explained that this therapy would probably never make it into mainstream medical care because even though it was very effective, no one is interested in using less medicine which would cut into profits for everyone in the business of cancer. It was as fascinating to hear about the complexity and simplicity of this therapy as it was about how it became a miraculous answer to the prayers for so many of the patients, who benefited from this unique and innovative approach. Within a few years, Rick became a master at IPT and used it to help countless of his patients find healing, although sadly, it would not be helpful for his own particular kind of lung cancer.

Later I introduced him to a pharmacist whose parents and much of his family died from various types of cancer, so he as well, was searching the world for innovative therapies and tests that would help humanity tame this unruly beast. He found a company in Germany, that would test the blood of a patient in a Petri dish against every possible medication and supplement that would effectively interact with the cancer. Once the most effective option was discovered, it was administered to the patient directly. Allowing for more accuracy, efficacy, and speed, than the old trial and error, wait and see approach. And when every minute counts this was a very powerful, albeit somewhat expensive procedure. Well, Rick became one of their top clients in the US, and again used this unique approach to figure out how to deliver the most effective outcomes.

For all those years, Rick kept searching and trying and testing everything that seemed like it had application and the most likely possibility to get to the root cause of chronic health problems so as to resolve them permanently. He used his experience, brilliance, and logic to identify and implement the most out of the box approaches he could find. Those usually way ahead of their time, and like every great scientist, he would first test these innovative products and services out on himself, before introducing them to his clients. Basically, he was doing what I imagine the great healers of history meant when they said that they were, 'practicing' medicine.

Unfortunately, these innovative, safe, and powerful therapies are not readily available in the United States. They are not FDA approved and are not covered by health insurance. Effectively they are only used by those doctors who are brave enough to draw boldly outside the standard-of-care box, and those patients who can afford to pay for them.

TOXIC THOUGHTS

On the wall of my auto-repair shop in the late 1980's I had a poster advertising the FRAM oil filter. Towards the bottom of the large photo of the orange filter there was the now famous tagline, that said "pay me now, or pay me later, but pay me you will." It was a popular commercial from a company that spared no expense educating the consumer on how to take better care of one of their largest investments, consistently since 1932. The idea was that if you spend a few dollars for a quality preventive measure now, you can avoid being forced to pay a mechanic to replace your car engine later, which always happens at the most inconvenient time, place, and cost.

Certainly, our bodies are quite more complex than the most complex vehicles on the road today, but they are also pretty simple. And unlike a mechanical creation of man, that must have experts fix it once it breaks down, the human body has the remarkable ability for self-regeneration. When you have a cut on your finger, it is not the band-aid that heals it, but the internal mechanism set in place by the Creator of this universe. Sometimes, of course, if we neglect, and indeed abuse this remarkable bio-machine, a tremendous amount of time and effort will be necessary to try and restore it back to high performance settings. Unfortunately changing parts within the human body is much more difficult and expensive than it would be on a mechanical vehicle, one that could be restored back to life no matter how old or damaged it is, if someone wanted to make that kind of investment.

The Russian people have a rhythmic saying, and one that I've heard many times over the years, it goes something like this: *"Who doesn't smoke or drink each day, will die healthy, anyway!"* It may seem like a harmless and amusing view of the world, but it was also responsible for the average Russian looking frighteningly old by their forties and then die not much later. I've watched many of the old guard pass away, by or just after, their sixtieth birthday, as they suffered all the diseases of the extremely aged for decades prior. Everyone seemed tough and impervious in their prime, but those years of youth click along fairly rapidly, and before you know it, you are living the decrepit nightmare born of neglect, abuse, apathy, and misinformation. But just because you don't know or understand gravity or physics and jump out of a vehicle moving at sixty miles per hour, you can't complain about the immutable laws that manifest the less than desirable, but eternally consistent outcome.

And, in this case as well, pleading ignorance is not a defense.

Later, when I learned some things about this concept of proactive wellness, I came up with my own answer to this nihilistic outlook. And said it enthusiastically whenever I heard anyone try to affirm this kind of self-destructive idea on what is usually a lovely and festive occasion. It went something like this: *"And those who poison themselves every day, spend a decade in bed, and then pass away."*

But let's not be too hard on the Russians, those poor people endured 70 years' worth of communism, and perhaps we can't fault them for not wanting to suffer any longer than necessary. In my current reality however, I sleep in a clean bed, I live in a warm house, I am not under relentless fear of being arrested or molested, I am free to do or say virtually anything I want, I don't have to worry about the safety of the people I love, and when it comes to food, my concern is having too much access, rather than too little. Life is good for even the average person, in this remarkable nation, and extraordinary time in the history of mankind.

On the other hand, walking into my favorite coffee shop this morning, I overheard two baristas exchanging greetings. "How are you" asked the petite young lady, who looked more like a second-grade schoolteacher relative to the scantily dressed, heavily tattooed barista with facial piercings, who she was addressing. "I'm suicidal bro, other than that I'm great" she answered stoically. So, clearly not everyone who lives in proximity, and who we consider fellow citizens, are doing well. Some are indeed so frustrated, so unwell, lonely, depressed, and stressed, that the idea of taking their own life is not an unlikely possibility. In fact, in 2022 the United States lost 49,449 people to suicide, a 5% increase over the year before. And this number excludes those who take the slightly slower route to their demise through chain smoking, alcohol abuse, gluttony, reckless driving, and illicit drugs.

And it is from this group of tortured humanity primarily that we get these destructive philosophies that permeate our lexicon. Ones we mouth like privileged teenagers do gangster rap at a fancy Bar Mitzvah. They tell us that we have to live for the moment, only the good die young, I hate exercise, I live for food, I'd rather spend my money on travel than prevention and wellness, I'll sleep when I'm dead, I don't need to supplement, I don't drink water, if it feels good do it, I don't want to be a health nut, rose' all day, being obese can be beautiful, I don't have any self-control for wellness, etc. etc.

Clearly, you and I are not those people. There is a mission that you are pursuing. Your ship is pointing towards the North Star, and you are putting in a tremendous amount of effort in getting yourself to the destination you've envisioned. But all those thoughts are the suffocating pollution that settles on our mind like a thick fog around your vessel, blocking your view, sapping your energy and turning you, even if for a moment, into the human tragedy from whom these thoughts originate.

But the worst and most damaging part of this verbal secondhand smoke, poisoning our thought process, is when we start purposely inhaling it, because it seems like everyone else is having such a great time doing it. When we begin repeating these chronic cliches, in just or in jest, is when they enter our consciousness like sugar flooding a cancer cell. Those philosophies begin to permeate our mind akin to a virus inserted into your computer directly via a thumb drive. Our mouth, as well, has a direct connection to our brain, and the words we utter is the most powerful way to program our subconscious mind. Whether it's by accident or on purpose, the actions we take will be congruent with the driving code we ourselves install, and the outcome we experience.

Those of us living our purpose and chasing our dream of raising a family, building a business or a career, and making a dent in the proverbial universe, can't afford to entertain these kinds of destructive thoughts not even for a minute. Especially in the early stages as you form your beliefs and life philosophy. Like a drop of water falling on granite, interacting with poisonous negativity once, may not cause much damage. But when it comes at you every day, those drops become a steady stream. Given enough time it will eventually cut through the toughest stone. In the same way self-destructive thoughts can undermine your ambition, creativity, and the very vessel that makes success, happiness, prosperity, and fulfillment possible.

The beliefs that drive our daily actions are made from the strands of those thoughts we permit to enter our mind and pass our lips. Eventually they are weaved into a perceived reality that nothing will likely be able to break and that will propel you down the path of chronic illness, obesity, and early demise.

Over 400 years ago, John Milton wrote the now eternal, Paradise Lost. Consisting of over 10,000 lines of poetic text, the one most often quoted is *"The mind is its own place and in itself can make a Heaven of Hell and a Hell of Heaven."* And although he was already blind when he began this epic project, he could clearly see that all happiness, success, and fulfilment live in our mind. I would just add that it is the thoughts that we allow to enter and permeate our thinking, solidified through daily affirmation that ultimately fosters how we see, and indeed experience the world.

MONEY, MONEY, MONEY …

If I could go back to when I was first diagnosed with psoriatic arthritis, I would give myself all kinds of advice, but perhaps the one I would lead with is the one I consider most important. Perhaps the most destructive and self-defeating idea I held was that someone else should pay for me to cure this chronic health issue, and that spending any money out of pocket is somehow foolish. In fact, a friend of mine who had a business selling health insurance at the time, shared a story of going to a doctor he was referred to who practiced unconventionally and did not accept any third-party payer reimbursement, but perhaps he would be able to help him avoid a surgery that he was scheduled to have.

"I spent a thousand dollars seeing this doctor and he was not able to help me anyway" he lamented. Wow, I remember thinking, a thousand dollars, that's a lot of money. So, over the years that's pretty much how I acted. When I ordered a supplement that cost fifty dollars, I always felt a bit guilty and somewhat dopey for spending money on something that may not help me, when I could have just as well bought a good bottle of wine and at least enjoy myself.

That seemed like it was somewhat more reasonable and acceptable.

But it was this hesitancy, this misunderstanding of the very purpose of money, and having so little faith in my own ability to effect positive change that kept me at the mercy of my own chronic illness for such a long time. One that was now threatening my very ability to live life, as the psoriasis continued expanding from one year to the next taking over some 60% of the real estate on my body, finally reaching the sides of my face.

It was bad enough that for some twenty years I was not able to take off my clothes in public and would usually sit at the beach during the hot summers like a religious woman in Tehran. Wearing a long-sleeved shirt and pants watching my friends play in the surf. Now I would not be able to show my face in public either. I'd be relegated to the eternal isolation of solitary confinement for the rest of my life.

Imprisoned in my own self.

If I understood that money was simply a tool, one that is specifically designed to get us the things we want and make life better and more interesting in the moment as well as in the future. Not a priceless family heirloom that you must protect at all costs and preserve for the next generation at the expense of your own wellbeing. A client of mine, who was one of the first holistic practitioners that reached out to participate in my conferences, spent forty years providing cause-focused care to his many patients. He was a chiropractor originally, but then got trained in clinical nutrition, psychotherapy and numerous other modalities that helped him create miracles, first for himself and later for his many patients.

The reason for his passionate pursuit of this kind of proactive medicine is a story I've heard so many times by now from other physicians in this burgeoning field of functional medicine. When he was a child, my doctor friend was diagnosed with some life-altering conditions, everything from scoliosis that required a titanium rod, psoriasis that covered 80% of his body, and made his hands bleed on the paper as he did his schoolwork. Perhaps the worst of his health problems, required numerous ambulance rides and emergency room visits, as he would fall into a diabetic coma and pass out on top of his desk while in class.

It would not be an interesting story if he did not resolve all those conditions. Never needing the titanium rod inserted in his spine, and then over the decades, helping countless of his clients drill down to the root of their chronic symptomatology and regain optimal function.

He shared a story with me about a client who came to see him. Although he did not tell me his name, he said that I would recognize who it was if he did. This was a famous billionaire living on the gold coast, in an exclusive neighborhood, and a palatal home in proximity to this wellness center. This middle-aged man was dealing with a chronic, and life-altering health problem that no one was able to help him with, and eventually in desperation found his way to this unique practitioner's office. What he told me was that during the first meeting, what this extremely wealthy man said, is that he is willing to do anything that this doctor recommended, so long as it was going to be paid by his health insurance plan. In other words, he was not willing to pay a dollar for the possibility of permanently resolving the bane of his existence, if he had to pay anything out of pocket for it.

What can one say to that?

So, it's ok to spend millions of dollars on a house, spare no expense on a collection of exotic cars, order custom made suits from exclusive tailors, drop a small fortune every time you go out to a restaurant, or stay at five-star hotels as you travel the world in luxury. Then have the wherewithal to invest other millions in real estate, stock market, and business ventures. But to allocate a few hundred dollars to someone with a lifetime of wisdom and expertise in helping you get to the root cause of a chronic condition, one threatening your very existence is somehow against your principles.

That is just outright lifestyle malpractice.

If those with virtually unlimited resources, and the kind of people we look up to as brilliant or even genius, because they were able to figure out how to make lots of money, are susceptible to this kind of bizarre, self-defeating reasoning, then what possible chance do the rest of us mere mortals have. Most people who say that they can't afford to pay for a doctor are mistaken. Perhaps they can't afford their house, or car, or jewelry, or branded clothing, primarily because they placed more value on those things than they did on their own existence, freedom, and quality of life.

It's sort of like the old story of how the native bushman sets a trap to catch a baboon. He first makes a hole in a giant ant heap, placing some wild melon seeds inside, while making sure the monkey is watching him do it. Then he goes off and hides, waiting for the curiosity of this very curious animal to hit a boiling point. Eventually the baboon runs up, places his hand in the narrow hole and grabs a fist full of seeds. Then when he tries to pull his hand out, it is the fist full of bounty, that does not allow him to escape, and he eventually becomes whatever his captor has in mind for him.

And usually, it's nothing good.

I've met lots of people who are saving for retirement, saving to leave an inheritance, saving for a rainy day, saving to buy a boat or a house or a car. All these things are great of course, but what are they worth if you are not able to enjoy them. They say that a person who is well has lots of dreams, but once they are sick, they have only one. Imagine for a moment what it would be like if you were diagnosed with some kind of a condition that does not allow you to take a walk outside because your joints hurt, or go to the beach because you have frightening lesions all over your skin, or eat the foods you love because it inflames your bowel and makes your condition erupt?

This changes everything.

Suddenly, all the dreams you once had, everything you considered important, even the people you lived for, none of it matters. Now the only thing you want, indeed everything you pray for or think about, is some kind of miracle so you can get well and get back to living your life like before. If you thought that taking care of your wellbeing, getting enough sleep, and placing the proverbial oxygen mask on yourself first was somehow selfish, you have no idea how selfish you can become when the air becomes so thin, that you are put in a position of having to fight for just one more breath.

ROAD LESS TRAVELED

Even though Rick and I were working together, and I was his sole marketing department, and I like to think friend, I still had to pay for all the blood tests, supplements, IV treatments, chelation therapies, and detoxification protocols out of pocket. None of it was covered by my "health" insurance and it was not cheap. I spent probably around fifteen thousand dollars over those three months. And I have to be honest, every time I put down my credit card to pay for yet another thing, I felt kind of foolish. As I kept thinking of my health-insurance friend who was indignant about having to pay a thousand dollars out of pocket for something that may not even be of any help.

Well, here I was spending many times that and with no certainty of having a positive outcome. But what I did have was hope. And putting what amounted to a significant sum of money for me, into getting the result I wanted, I believe bent the universe into making what I demanded of it happen. The decision to put my money where my mouth is, turned regular hope from a noun into an adjective, its proactive, and more powerful version. Now, I realize that for some it may seem like a crazy thing to spend so much money, for something we're told should be free. In fact, many of my friends and family told me so in no uncertain terms. For others it may seem like nothing, as one of the doctors I worked with, who was dealing with some disruptive health issues, spent a quarter of a million dollars going to functional doctors around the country before she found the spontaneous remission miracle she sought.

There was no change for most of those ninety days, and I'm not sure how much longer I would have been able to finance this kind of ostentatious extravagance. But then, within a week, the pain subsided as if someone turned a switch, and now twenty years later, it never came back. And although the psoriasis remained and continued to get worse from one year to the next, I think it's worth acknowledging that permanently resolving the arthritis part of this devastating diagnosis was one of those personal miracles worthy of the most reverent kind of gratitude.

Here I believed that for psoriatic arthritis, there was no cure. Because that's what the experts told me time and again. And if there was, you could only find it in a drug created by the genus scientist who works for one of the large pharmaceutical companies and prescribed by a medical doctor board certified by some impressive sounding academy. But definitely, it could not be found by a doctor, who some mainstream medical groups would call a 'quack', because he left the reservation and was no longer practicing 'real' medicine. And certainly not by paying so much money for it out of pocket, instead of going through the "health" insurance company that, as everyone knows, has my best interest at heart and is happy to pay for everything I may need.

Because they care so very much.

Coincidently, a friend and neighbor of ours, who lives literally around the corner, was diagnosed with rheumatoid arthritis, shortly after my recovery. A lovely woman, a few years younger than me, she was an executive with one of the software companies in midtown making north of two hundred and fifty thousand dollars per year. Slightly under five feet tall, what she lacked in stature she more than made up in toughness and hutzpah. I remember a specific moment when she stood in the basement of the Copacabana, a nightclub that was opened in 1940 and named after the famous beach in Rio de Janeiro, pointing her finger at the face of a well-dressed manager who must have been seven feet tall, demanding a refund.

I organized a trip for five of our couple friends to celebrate Valentines Day, purchased tickets on their website, and after waiting in a long line for like an hour in the freezing cold, we were finally let in passed the velvet rope and entered the club. It was so packed in there that there was no place to even stand. The coat room was completely full, the bars had crowds ten people deep, and the dance floor packed with thousands of people dancing and sweating and moving and spinning as the Latin music blared through the human sized speakers in virtually every corner. There we stood in our winter coats, the ladies clutching their purses with both hands, as people tried to squeeze past us in one direction or another. They oversold this evening by at least a thousand people and after we stood there for some time, trying to look like we were having fun, she stormed to the registration desk demanding to see the manager.

Long story short, they refunded our money, and we went someplace quiet for dinner where we could finally relax and have some laughs recounting how our fearless warrior princess had to almost get on her tippy toes so the giant manager would notice her, as she delivered her very convincing point.

She went to see Rick, after I told her about my experience, but after paying five hundred dollars for that initial consultation, she told me that there is no way she is paying that kind of money when she has access to the "best" doctors in the country through her top-tier health insurance. The last time I saw her was about 10 years ago, and she was already on full disability and could barely move or get out of bed, even though she was taking chemo-like drugs, and the strongest pain medication available, prescribed by those infallible doctors.

I just can't help but wonder what would have happened if she as well took the road less traveled.

So, I was fortunate to find my way to healing from a debilitating condition that would have surely ruined my life and bankrupted my family if I did not choose to stay off the beaten path. And although I had to deal with the psoriasis part of that diagnosis for some 20 years since, recently I found the answer to its permanent resolution as well.

We'll discuss that a bit later in the book.

And so, if there was a way to permanently resolve what is a life destroying chronic health problem, how much better would it be to never have gotten it in the first place? I mean, if it could be cured, as it were then certainly it would be much easier to prevent it from manifesting in the first place.

Wouldn't you think?

But I'm not sure human nature is ready for such perfection. Remember, how in the first Matrix movie, Agent Smith was explaining to Morpheus as he sat tied to a chair, that the first program the system created to keep humanity placated was designed as a perfect human world, where none suffered, and where everyone would be happy. *"It was a disaster. It seems that as a species humans define their reality through misery and suffering."* he concluded.

Perhaps he is right and much of the evidence seems to point to the fact that he may very well be. But I truly hope not, and that perhaps we can still find some awake and rebellious people out there, who want to circumvent illness and extend lifespan. Because I've dedicated my life to this being true, and my entire Science of Human Optimization business model is betting on that debatable possibility.

~

FINAL THOUGHT

"It is health that is real wealth and not pieces of
gold and silver." – *Mahatma Gandhi*

Chapter 7

SCIENCE OF HUMAN OPTIMIZATION

Precision Care for High Performance Individuals.

Unlike an airplane, or race car, the human body does not come with gauges so we can know what's happening behind the scenes, and under the hood. We have no idea when some of the life-supporting nutrients become depleted, or when our detoxification pathways become overwhelmed, or when our digestion is compromised, or when there is a spark that ignites systemic inflammation. Once we develop very early-stage symptoms like a skin rash, bumpy fingernails, bleeding gums, poor sleep, hair loss, allergies, inexplicable weight gain, digestion problems, joint pain, bad breath, brain fog, or headaches. We will usually ignore it or take an over-the-counter medication to try to ameliorate the condition, numb the discomfort, and hopefully feel better.

Eventually when the symptoms become uncomfortable enough, we'll dig out the health insurance card and go visit an in-network doctor. For the most part, those providers who accept your health insurance will examine you briefly, usually just a few minutes, and most likely prescribe a stronger medication to address the complaint and numb the complainer. And although there is no out of pocket cost per se, this approach offers a temporary fix at best, and suppresses and pressurizes the very cause of a health catastrophe, at worst.

Wellness Walk

When my son was about five years old, he was dealing with chronic ear infections to the point that his hearing was affected. His English tutor pointed this out to us after one of the lessons, as she put a hand over her mouth, so he would not see her lips move, and called him by his name. My wife and I both heard her clearly, but he did not.

Evey time we would come back from the pediatrician; he was given a stronger prescription for an antibiotic to fill. Even then it felt a little strange that a child was getting an adult dose of medication, while the problem was consistently getting worse. Eventually the doctor recommended ear tube surgery, called Tympanostomy. It's a very common and relatively simple procedure, he reassured, as small hollow plastic tubes are inserted into the eardrum, to constantly drain the fluid from the ears.

It just so happened that the doctor was headed for vacation the following week and offered to perform the surgery when he came back. By then I had met some really interesting doctors, and a few who practiced something called Chiropractic. *"A profession that works with that subtle substance of the soul, that tiny rivulet of force that emanates in the mind, flows over the nerves to the cells and stirs them to life"* as the founder of this idealistic healing philosophy so eloquently explained. I worked in a medical office in Brooklyn, where one young doctor kept after me to have me try an adjustment that he was performing on dozens of people who came for treatment daily. After witnessing a few of his hands-on therapies, where the person would lie on their back on a special table, and the doctor would twist their neck until an audible popping would emanate that sounded like bones cracking. And although I never took him up on his offer at the time, after a couple of years of being around these remarkable people and learning the origins of this interesting profession, I became a fan and would go for regular weekly treatments myself.

Back in 1895, BB Palmer performed what is considered the very first chiropractic treatment on the janitor who worked in his building and had lost his hearing 17 years prior after being injured in an accident.

This is Harvey Lillard's recounting of the events:

"Palmer told me that my deafness came from an injury in my spine. This was new to me; but it is a fact that my back was injured at the time I went deaf. Dr. Palmer treated me on the spine; in two treatments I could hear quite well. That was eight months ago. My hearing remains good."

CAN YOU HEAR ME NOW

Speaking with Dr. Edward Acevedo, a chiropractor I met while working in his office in Jackson Heights, I shared with him my son's condition and my frustration with the treatment protocol. He suggested that before I agree to the surgery that I bring him for an evaluation. After the initial exam, Dr. Acevedo suggested we schedule the boy to come in three times per week for a month, so that he could adjust his neck and spine regularly.

After that course of unconventional treatment, my adorable five-year-old's hearing was fully restored, the ear infections went away permanently, and we never went back to the pediatrician who suggested surgery. My daughter who is a few years younger than my son, had immediate chiropractic treatments when she developed her first ear infection, and we did not have to go through the same drama with her as we did with the boy.

Over the years I've met many medical doctors (MD's and DO's) as well, who practiced a more proactive approach, and would have to do it outside the established medical system and the third-party payers that control it. They all have their individual reasons for leaving to practice on their own terms, but usually it's because they or someone they love developed a chronic health problem and were not able to find a solution in the indefinite management of chronic disease (IMCD) industrial complex.

Although one physician I know, Erika Schwarts, MD who has a lovely center in NYC, happens to cater to some of the wealthiest people in the world, and is the author of *Don't Let Your Doctor Kill You: How to Beat Physician Arrogance, Corporate Greed, and a Broken System*, was insulted when a patient left a five-dollar co-payment on her desk in the early days of her private practice. When she understood that this was how the system worked, she immediately left all the insurance plans and started practicing for the 'cash on the barrel model', of direct payments only.

But regardless of their reasons for leaving the *reservation*, or if we accept the Merriam-Webster definition of 'a system for the cure of disease based on dogma set forth by its promulgator', then perhaps we can say, leaving the *cult*. These brave doctors begin walking a very tight rope of doing what they believe is right under the threat of persecution, demonization, and cancellation. They also have to go for extensive training in functional medicine, and travel to conferences around the world to learn from a handful of pioneers in the field. Where before all they had to do was make sure they were in the thick directory of a particular insurance plan, and that was enough for people to beat a path to their door. At the same time, they had to become a salesperson, business expert, and marketing professional. Spending another fortune getting their message out to enough people to hopefully find those few who can see past the "healthcare should be free" paradigm and experience the benefits of this kind of personalized, proactive, and cause-focused care for themselves.

Should you get frustrated enough with the standard of care in our current medical system, perhaps you too will find your way to a functional medicine doctor. For the most part this small but growing group of remarkable physicians do not accept health insurance. They do, however, take the time to try and understand how to resolve the underlying cause of the symptoms presented. Using supplements, innovative therapies, cutting edge technology, lifestyle modification, and at times medication. Because they operate outside the multi-trillion-dollar (IMCD) industrial complex, the cost of seeing this kind of doctor represents all the additional training, liberal diagnostic time, personal risk, and financial investment which can be substantial, but perhaps the outcome will be more satisfactory and longer lasting for the individual consumer.

The trouble with either option however, the allopathic or functional, is that they are only engaged once the symptom, (usually the result of deficiency, toxicity, or a compromised system of digestion) has evolved significantly enough to be distracting to the point of demanding action. Once you are sitting in front of them, they have a very limited time to get to know the many varying aspects of the unique case that you present, as they try to find the best option from their individual therapeutic paradigm. Even the hour or two that the functional physicians allocate for the initial consultation still offers a limited view of the genetics, nutrition, blood chemistry, toxicity, and lifestyle factors that contribute to the underlying cause or a chronic symptom, as well as lifespan potential.

Sadly, by the time most people hear about any of the 'alternative' options like chiropractic, naturopathic, functional medicine, nutritionist, acupuncture, or Science of Human Optimization they have been to virtually every allopathic option on the planet and are now dealing with a situation that could only be labeled as desperate.

UNICORNS & RAINBOWS

When you pour water into a cup it takes the form of the cup, spill it on the floor and it takes the form of the tile. The context that is the cup gives shape to the content that is the water. When I speak with experts in the field of healthcare, they all agree that the system is unsustainable, too bureaucratic, redundant, secretive, and "broken". But usually offer to fix some aspect of the content (the water) without addressing the context (the cup). Expanding access by passing a government sponsored insurance option into law for example. Cracking down on the rampant and ubiquitous fraud within the Medicare and Medicaid circles. Passing a law to make pricing among the hospital systems more transparent. Engaging HMOs to try and reduce cost from the top down. These are all worthwhile endeavors I suppose.

But that's about as effective as warming your tooshie with a match to survive an avalanche.

Our system of health care, one modeled on the European one-payer, government controlled, altruistic system of unicorns and rainbows. One caked with layers of bureaucratic fixes is unaffordable, unsustainable, and unattractive. Perpetuated over the last seven decades of glutenous consumption, resembling Jabba the Hut from Star Wars fame, it has grown into a morbidly obese blob, fighting for each breath while being crushed under its own girth of impracticality. As it gorges itself on an all you can eat buffet of backroom deals, special interest kickbacks, and under-the-table handoffs.

To challenge it directly or to attempt to fix it would be a fool's errand as its only possible trajectory is to grow bigger. And then much bigger still. Our only refuge is that we live in the United States of America. Where ingenuity and creativity, and freedom of thought has permitted innovative entrepreneurs to create better options to the systems that are in decline. No matter how big, wealthy, well established, corrupt, deeply connected or entrenched they may be.

Eventually they all crumble and give way to the better model.

BASIC ECONOMICS

Not long after we arrived in this country, I made my first significant purchase with some of the American dollars I saved selling packs of Wriggles gum door to door in the building complex where we lived. It was a vinyl album of The Police, a British-American new wave band, that I bought in a large record store on Main Street, about 30-minute walk from where we lived. I vividly remember how the cashier gently slid the magnificent cover into a thin brown paper bag and handed it to me. When I got home, I carefully removed the packaging and placed the album on the secondhand record player that my parents salvaged and repaired. Then meticulously lowered the needle onto the starting groove, and for the first time heard how Roxanne no longer had to put on the red light. I of course did not understand what they were singing, as I did not speak the language, or the meaning behind the words, even if I did, but the feeling of that music touched my soul.

This was late 1979 at the very peak of the vinyl industry market share, at some 54 billion dollars per year it was the undisputed champion of the music business, growing consistently for the 25 years prior. Then in 1984 it was significantly disrupted when cassette tapes became the favorite option.

They were smaller, more portable and you can listen to them through your car radio, boombox, or Walkman virtually anywhere. Later the cassette was made obsolete when James Russel, the American physicist and music lover invented the compact disk, which took over the market as the favorite way of storing and listening to music in the early 1990s.

This is the natural way for the market to transition from business models and technology that become obsolete in the face of innovation and advancements. There are many more such examples, like fax machines and email, propellers and jet engines, carburetors and fuel injection, tokens and EZ pass, as well as typewriters and laptops to name a few. Once a better approach is introduced, the market usually adopts, morphs, and available resources change hands. People get laid off from one industry and are hired by another, office space is vacated by one group and leases signed by another, raw materials get redirected from the old way of doing things to the new.

It is very different in our system of care, however, as the heavy hand of the government creates what is known as crony capitalism. Forming a profitable and perverse 'quid pro quo' relationship between bureaucrat and business. A web or intertwined special interests that undermines the natural laws of economics and replaces them with elitist ideas pushed by the likes of the now infamous Jonathon Gruber. Considered the architect of Obama Care, he is the MIT professor of economics who famously said that it was because of the "stupidity of the American voter" that the healthcare bill needed to be presented in a tortured way. And that it was the lack of transparency that permitted the unaffordable ACA to become law. So, he was willing to obfuscate, lie, and misinform the very 'of the people' by whom this government is supposedly run, because HE would rather have this law than not.

But anytime you force this kind of imperial imposition via decree between the public and a service business, it always creates unintended consequences that no one wants, and that later, no one will take responsibility for. In his brilliant and voluminous book with a simple cover, called Basic

Economics, Thomas Sowell expands on this phenomenon of unintended consequences, saying:

"Under a government-run medical system the government can at any given time set medical salary scales, or pay scales for particular medical treatments, which are not sufficient to continue to attract as many people of the same qualifications into the medical profession in the future."

According to a recent article in Epoch Times, called "Why America's Physician Shortage is Getting Worse" author Autumn Spredemann, explains that burnout and early retirement is resulting in a scarcity of doctors. As the ones who remain will have to pick up the slack, making the situation worse. In fact, it's projected that the United States will face a shortage of 124,000 doctors by 2034 in primary care, surgery, and other specialties. So, in other words, the expense of our system of health care grows exponentially, while the quality, value, and access falls precipitously.

But that's ok, perhaps our government can fast-track a new generation of 'doctors' from the ranks of those who recently crossed the Rio Grande and hopped over the fence.

IT'S NOT ALL IN YOUR MIND

It was about six years ago when I gained twenty pounds inexplicably for the second time in the last twenty years. Shortly after the first time I was diagnosed with psoriatic arthritis. Although my diet and exercise regimen remained the same, I could no longer fit into any of my suits or slacks. One thing I was certain about is that this time, I was not going to see a doctor who took my health insurance. Because by then I was thoroughly convinced that I was not interested in that type of one-size-fits-all, public clinic, numb the symptom, 'cattle care'.

Fortunately for me, a couple of serendipitous events happened, at virtually the same time. First, a doctor of osteopathy who just sold her allopathic medical practice and opened a small concierge center reached out to me to help her market it. She was dealing with a chronic health problem for years that neither her education, approach, nor medical network was able to solve. Only after seeing a functional medicine doctor herself was she able to find permanent relief. Once she experienced that spontaneous remission miracle, she could no longer practice in good faith, the disease management model that she was taught in medical school and spent 20 years providing.

Not long after that, someone referred the marketing director of a start-up software company, called Integrative Genetic Solutions (IGS) that did something I had never heard of till that point in time. Foundered by a real-life renaissance man considered a mathematical child prodigy. Graduating from college at the age of 19, he then served as a Green Barret in the US military, and later studied to be a field surgeon, graduating second in his class. Jonathan Orban ran one of the largest companies in the nation, before he was injured, that designed computer programs for banks. So, if it took a month to process a loan manually, he and his team would create software that would crunch the numbers in minutes.

One of his favorite pastime activities was bicycle racing, and it was during one of those marathons on wheels through Alaska, that he was hit by a van, and almost killed. He woke up in a hospital after extensive surgery, with 17 pins, plates, bolts, and screws on the left side of his body. And after months of rehabilitation, although he regained his ability to walk, his health began a downward spiral. Gaining 30 pounds inexplicably he was chronically exhausted, and unable to think clearly. To the point that he needed to write down where he parked his car, losing the cognitive ability that allowed him to perform complicated mathematics in his mind.

Like everyone else, Jon first took his excellent 'health' insurance card and went to see the 'top specialists' around the country. Even if he thought there was the smallest chance of them being able to help in his recovery. Everyone who did his labs came to virtually the same conclusion, all the markers were normal, and they did not see anything wrong. Except one doctor, who explained that it was probably because he was getting older, and it was just the natural aspect of the body slowing down.

For someone who was then in his thirties, and one of the top ten finishers in ultra extreme races just a few months prior, this did not compute. Especially that now he was processing this hypothesis through some serious brain fog. Reaching out to his large network of business, athlete, military, and medical contacts, the one name that kept coming up was one of the top human chemistry experts in the nation. A doctor by the name of Richard Lee, who was a professor at Stanford, spent 25 years in the field, and ran a very exclusive concierge practice.

Over the years, I've met doctors who are so exclusive, and effective, it's not uncommon for them to charge six figures plus to take on a case. And although we're made to think that everyone is equal in the eyes of our system of care with identical access for any person with an insurance card. Believe me when I tell you, it's not. Those with the resources, work with the kind of doctors most of us will never get to see, even as a hallucination. So, when Jon says he wrote him a big check, I can only imagine how big the check was.

After doing all his labs, and genetic tests and every other high-tech assessment protocol at his disposal, Jon was placed on a very specific regimen of vitamins, therapies, and medications. And within a month he felt like his old self, and within six months he was back on the podium in racing competitions. Most importantly he was once again able to tap his cognitive skills.

So, after that experience, Jon went back to Dr. Lee with a proposal. What if we took everything you and other doctors of your caliber know about human chemistry and design a computer program that will correlate all that information with an individual person's blood work. It will come up with very narrow guidelines and will be kind of like, coloring by the numbers, allowing virtually any practitioner to easily follow along. This will democratize exclusive and very expensive concierge medicine and make it available to anyone interested in living a longer and healthier life.

Well, like virtually everything else I introduce to the public, I must first try it on myself. I reached out to that doctor of osteopathy with the new practice and asked her to put me through this IGS program. The phlebotomist showed up at my house and collected, no exaggeration, at least 20 vials of my blood. It took about a month to get the results to my doctor, and we met over zoom to go over them for about an hour. From what I recall, my vitamin D was below 20 ng/mL, I was not absorbing my vitamin C, my testosterone was low, my estrogen was high, my homocysteine was way above normal, and there was another 20 or so things that were highlighted as out of balance and brought to my attention. Once my doctor made her own adjustments and suggestions, the report was forwarded to a compounding pharmacy that formulated all the supplements and the bio-identical hormones that came in the mail some weeks later.

After taking all the vitamins and administering the creams for about a month, the 20 pounds that I gained inexplicably, came off without me doing anything different, other than fixing my chemistry. But then the things I experienced were as surprising as they were miraculous.

First, my brain-fog lifted.

For almost two years I was walking around not able to think straight, I could not tap my creativity, I did not show up for meetings, got lost in presentations, and forgot to return calls. It was awful, but somewhere in the back of my mind I thought that now that I'm in my mid-forties, maybe that is what getting older feels like. I was also chronically fatigued, and it seemed like no matter how long I slept each night I was thoroughly exhausted during the day. And probably because my hormones were upside down, I was super sensitive and would be 'hurt' and become petulant by the smallest slight or rejection. It's tough to run a business and organize conferences with thousands of people when you have such 'thin skin' all of a sudden. Well, all that changed in a relatively short time, and I got to experience the remarkable power of human optimization firsthand.

All of this is anecdotal of course, and there were no double-blind studies to prove this account, so you know, take it with a grain of salt. But since we're talking here, and we both agree that it can just be some kind of a placebo effect, let me just add this little gem. For a few years prior to this optimization program, my eyes were getting fuzzy. I could no longer see the text in the books I was reading clearly. Since my mom got reading glasses in her forties, and it seemed like all my friends could no longer see what was written on the menu when we went out to a restaurant, I just thought that it was time to go see the optometrist to get myself fitted for some smart looking spectacles.

Low and behold, my sight came back stronger than before. Today I'm fifty-five years old, and praise the Lord, I'm typing this book on a small screen and tiny font size without prosthetics. Putting all this aside, when you optimize the body, and provide it with all the important chemistry that makes it work optimally, the results may just be very surprising, and it's reasonable to imagine that anything is possible.

Having said all this, I think it's important to manage expectations, as just because you don't feel anything happening does not mean that nothing is. It's like going on a long drive with a slight leak in your oil pan. Chances are you will never notice that your car is low on engine oil, and you won't feel anything when you add the quart or two that was missing, either. But should that oil get below a certain threshold eventually the damage will be as severe as it is inevitable. So even though you did not 'feel anything' when you added the necessary but depleted ingredient, you most certainly saved yourself a whole host of unpleasantries.

THE ART OF SELLING THE ART OF HEALING

When I first started hosting wellness conferences I noticed an interesting phenomenon. Medical doctors, with an MD after their name would usually get the best attendance at their lectures compared to any other degree. I found it somewhat amusing when the doctor speaking had virtually no idea about functional medicine, nutrition, or wellness. In comparison to the speaker in the next room who literally spent their entire adult life studying and practicing how to get to the root cause of a chronic illness rather than simply managing symptoms with pharmaceuticals. They may have had Naturopathic Doctor (ND) as their title, but somehow this group was suspect in the minds of the great masses. Sadly, this remarkable group of dedicated professionals are not even licensed in New York as of this writing and must practice in stealth, like a health coach with a weekend certificate, rather than the true doctors and healers they are. Having spent a similar amount of time studying biology, chemistry, and anatomy as a medical doctor, Naturopaths focused much more attention and time on nutrition, herbs, supplements, and other natural substances that could address the underlying cause and restore the body to optimal function.

On May 2-3 of 2020 we had our largest conference planned, with some 80 speakers flying in from all over the country, about 150 exhibitors and thousands of people scheduled to attend. Our keynote speaker was the seven-time NYT bestselling author Joel Fuhrman, MD one day, and David Minkoff, MD who completed 42 Iron Man Triathlons and wrote a book called *The Search for the Perfect Protein*, on the other. Well, you know how that went. My team and I started producing this event six months prior, and over the years had to deal with hurricanes, floods, black outs, and every challenge imaginable, so 'two weeks to flatten the curve' in March was not going to slow us down.

A few months prior, an interesting doctor reached out to me with a title I've never heard of till that point. She was a Family Nurse Practitioner (FNP), with a doctorate in nursing. We first met in NYC at a conference my team and I produced in November of 2019, and it was there, standing on the exhibit floor, she explained to me that she owned an anti-aging wellness practice in Brooklyn, and wanted to see if I would be willing to help her market it. I never worked with a Family Nurse Practitioner, and had no idea if the public would accept this professional the way they usually stood at attention and habitually disrobed for an MD. But she seemed nice, knowledgeable, passionate, and attractive.

Which, you know, never hurts.

First becoming a nurse at the age of 16 in Soviet Russia, and then coming to the United States with her husband and children some years later. Here she had to recertify everything and in a different language, and eventually worked for large medical institutions around New York. Years later she was diagnosed with some chronic health issues herself and could find no resolution in the established (IMCD) industrial complex.

As I said, I heard this story many times, and in many variations over the years.

We drew up an agreement in early 2020 and I featured her at a doctor-only dinner event we produced in Smithtown NY on March fifth, with David Katz, MD, author of *How to Eat*, as the keynote speaker. The plan was to feature her in our publication, and then introduce her as one of the main presenters at the larger conference in May, using that event as the springboard to further marketing.

I ended up hosting the entire weekend conference on zoom, a computer program that I never used before. And what can I say, it was a mitigated disaster that I don't like to think about. But from that moment I began to use this tool for virtual video conferencing and webinars where I would host the two doctors who stayed with me even though I was in all practical terms out of business.

Over those next couple of months I lost some 150 clients, many of whom I've worked with for over 15 years and considered friends. This was nothing personal of course, and I understood that logically, although emotionally being systemically fired by everyone simultaneously and for no fault of mine, was the most painful experience of my life. Shortly after that, and for the third time in the last two decades, I gained an inexplicable 20 pounds, and braised myself for the next health misadventure.

THE MISSING LINK

One of my frustrations as I produced these ScHO conferences and positioned all those functional medicine doctors in front of the public, was that no matter how hard I tried, some doctors were just not able to translate any of those people in their lecture room into paying clients. A handful of course, built very successful practices that generated millions of dollars in revenue, but for the most part, these doctor-entrepreneurs participated in my events simply to get their name out, and because it was the thing to do. But their ability to sell and get people committed to a program that was profitable enough to cover their expenses, was just not usually their strength.

That is one of the reasons why insurance companies and the pharmaceutical industry, who command an army of sales professionals with bespoke suits and low-cut dresses, are able to get people to sign self-defeating contracts on the dotted line, and with their own blood.

This unwelcome disruption to my business allowed a unique opportunity for me to understand what I considered the missing link in my business model. I wanted to see firsthand how the doctor/client interaction worked in a direct pay center model. So, for the next eight or so months I traveled to downtown Brooklyn to work in the center of my doctor FNP client so that I could understand this mysterious dynamic, and perhaps help improve patient flow. First, I bought a list of local business contacts that would make a good potential referral source, and then began calling and sending letters inviting them to visit our wellness center and meet my doctor. Even though this was the height of the COVID hysteria, with the little dictators forcing all kinds of restrictions and mandates, making the environment much more difficult to operate in, but despite that, eventually prospective clients began to make appointments.

Early on, a couple came in for an assessment. They spent over an hour with the doctor, and after they left, I asked her if they paid for the initial consultation. She looked a bit flustered, and then explained that they were young, and they did not have much money, and that she felt bad, etc. There was a lot of that kind of thing. She was a kind, beautiful, caring soul, trying to save the world and nurse people back to health, practicality and profit be damned. It was after seeing this kind of unsustainable dynamic time and again, I decided that there must be a way to share the labor based on the strengths of the individual.

The doctor needs to do the healing, I reasoned, and someone else needs to do the selling.

UNBREAKABLE

It was sometime in the summer of 2022, my wife and I had to go to some formal business function, when I realized that COVID shrunk all my suits. This was the third time that I inexplicably gained 20 pounds and by then I thought this was just utterly ridiculous. Why do I need to fall into these pits of malfunction and then seek some expert who would hopefully help me climb back out? Is it not a much better option to create the infrastructure to at least try and keep me out of them in the first place? And, preferably for the rest of my life, however long that happens to be.

When I placed an advertisement on a recruitment site looking for an FNP interested in functional medicine, I had almost two thousand candidates express interest who sent me their CV's and video introductions. Honestly, I was very surprised at the response, but as I began explaining to them what I was looking to do on our zoom interviews, I could see the light die in their eyes, even though they said they were interested in a more proactive approach to care.

Most of them were just looking for a better paying job and did not much care what it was, as long as it had good benefits and acceptable terms. Clearly, they were frustrated with the current system, and shared some stories about how they were treated over the last few years, but what I was explaining to them seemed as foreign as perhaps when someone gives me detailed driving directions in a country where I don't understand the language.

Eventually I found three Family Nurse Practitioners who seemed excited to do this with me, and as soon as I signed a few clients willing to try our program, I assigned them to my newfound ScHO team. Sadly, one of the younger practitioners bowed out just three months later because of some personal problems, the second one called me about a year into the program to say she was overwhelmed by family responsibilities and her fulltime job. But the one who proved herself unbreakable is Ilene Castaldo, who also happens to have been the most seasoned and experienced in functional medicine, and life.

The reason I chose family nurse practitioners (FNP) to lead the charge of human optimization, is because after these remarkable, and naturally caring people, first spent two years studying anatomy, microbiology, and chemistry to become a registered nurse. Most of those I interviewed also worked as providers for years before applying for additional training. Some worked in emergency rooms, obstetrics, women's health, and oncology. In fact, when my ScHO Practitioner found out that I never went, and don't plan to go for a colonoscopy. Even though I was older than fifty and even though I recently lost my little brother to colon cancer. She very calmly shared her experience of working in a cancer ward for five years of her nursing career. Gently and lovingly helping change my mind to do what was ultimately in my own best interest.

I'm happy to report that the procedure was uneventful, and I received a clean bill of health.

The process of becoming a nurse practitioner requires another two to four years of additional schooling, with some 500 clinical hours of study. They get deeper into interpretation of labs, understanding diagnostic data, and disparate therapeutics, with a focus on becoming wellness advocates for their clients. Once certified and licensed, most states allow the FNP to practice autonomously, and are trusted to cater to the health needs of millions of people throughout our nation.

That is an amazing foundation, in knowledge and experience, for us to then introduce them to the additional training required to become a ScHO Practitioner. This educational process is rigorous and continuous for the rest of their career, as we introduce them to the world's experts in human optimization, ageless beauty, and youthful longevity, with a focus on understanding genetics, blood-work interpretation, digestive biome, and toxicity. Our mission is to become the world's expert in the complex makeup of the individual client we're working with, and then use the most cutting-edge information from the top scientists, functional medicine doctors, and leading diagnostic experts to design the structures for life at its peak level of health expression.

Over the last twenty years I have been to all the top doctors to try and resolve the psoriasis that was threatening to destroy my life. As I mentioned, last year it started to expand to the sides of my face, and I've seen what people who were literally covered from head to toe looked like, on posters and brochures that very first day in the dermatologist's office, all those years ago. It was only after working with Ilene Castaldo, my ScHO Practitioner for just over a year, that we were able to identify and correct the underlying cause.

During the last few months, the lesions that covered some 60% of my body began to recede, and for the first time in twenty years the condition stopped progressing.

$\sim$

FINAL THOUGHT

"There are two ways to live: you can live as if nothing is a miracle; you can live as if everything is a miracle." – Albert Einstein

Chapter 8

PSORIASIS

My Twenty-Year Journey to a Ninety-Day Cure.

There is of course no cure for psoriasis, he said as a matter-of-factly, but you can manage the symptoms with these fancy creams and vitamins we developed specifically for this purpose. And with that, and a smile, he proceeded to place three large sample boxes into a bag with the logo of his company on the side.

Gingerly handing it to me.

The Integrative Healthcare Symposium (IHS) is an annual conference in NYC that I've been attending since its founding in 2005 and shortly after my own diagnosis. It attracts thousands of top functional medicine doctors from around the world. There are presentations by the more extraordinary physicians throughout the four-day event, as well as some 300 exhibiting companies who introduce cutting-edge technology and products that actually look to get to the root cause of chronic symptomatology.

After the initial niceties, the conversation became somewhat heated as I began to challenge this defeatist notion. Why did someone selling what is a natural supplement and cream, with admittedly impressive before and after photos of satisfied clients, feel compelled to say, that 'there is no cure to this skin condition' one affecting some eight million people in the United States?

First Bite

Well, even if the skin clears after some kind of therapy, he reasoned, it can still come back. So then it's not cured, he concluded, visibly frustrated. Sure, I answered, but if you scrape your knee and it heals, and then you scrape it again in the same spot weeks later, does it mean that the first time it healed, that it was not 'cured' as it were? Perhaps in the medical paradigm of symptom suppression this is truer, as when you stop the intervention the problem inevitably resurfaces, and most likely worse than before, because the underlying cause was not effectively addressed. But as far as I'm concerned, my arthritis was cured some 20 years ago, my brain fog was cured, my chronic fatigue, emotional instability, and now the incurable psoriasis as well, all have been cured. And as long as I continue keeping my body optimized, I contend that it will remain so, until the day my journey here concludes.

The 'there is no cure' mantra is very profitable for the multi trillion-dollar med-matrix, as once you're shackled with this belief chances are that you'll continue to find evidence to support it in everything you see and hear, and as decades pass, what was an angel hair of an idea becomes an iron harness of certainty. This insidious concept of "don't say cure" originated in the (IMCD) industrial complex and is imposed by the government on the supplement and functional medicine industries under the 'False Claims Act' that comes with some complex perimeters, and austere repercussions.

YOUR VERY BEST FRIEND

When I first met Ilene Castaldo, she did not strike me as a likely candidate to become the senior Science of Human Optimization Practitioner. As she did not have a headshot, virtually no social media presence, and she was not as flowery in her responses and communications as some of the other Nurse Practitioners I interviewed who expressed interest in working with us. But what she lacks in presentation and market presence, she more than makes up for in experience, intuition, compassion, courage, and healing prowess. It's been just over a year since we began working together, and during that time we did my blood work, genetic testing, as well as my digestive biome, and toxicity levels. We interviewed and consulted with some of the top functional medicine doctors and scientists from around the nation, and we did numerous detox protocols for my liver, lymph, and system of digestion.

Finally, it was about three months ago, that I felt like someone turned off the high-pressure water flow to the proverbial fire hose, and my skin exhaled and calmed for the first time in some twenty years. From that moment the psoriasis stopped flaking and the lesions on my skin began to recede at a rapid pace and like never before. Keeping in mind that over 60% of my body was covered with giant patches of scaling plaque, consistently expanding from one year to the next, encroaching onto virtually every body part at a geometric rate, making this, a spontaneous remission miracle worthy of reverent acknowledgment and pious gratitude.

Ever since I can remember, the experts have been telling me that my health problems are the result of my own immune system attacking itself. That never made sense. Where in nature does something attack when not provoked to attack? There are always reasons, causes, motives, and motivations even in the most unlikely outliers. The wolf attacks a lamb because he is hungry. Man attacks another a man because he was insulted or threatened. A bunch of women get into a brawl in the middle of a mall with hair pulling and face punching because ... actually, that's a mystery. But I intuitively know that one of your body systems does not simply attack itself for no reason, there must be something that either insulted it, or that it recognized as a threat. Believing that a part of your body is an enemy that you need to wage war against is a terrible paradigm. However long you've been alive, your immune system has been your very best friend, protecting you to the best of its ability, in a hostile environment and with limited resources, becoming more so from one year to the next.

Like me, approximately 150 million people in the US have the MTHFR gene making it difficult for them to detoxify the many assaults of the modern environment. That means that our biology did not evolve to live in this toxic soup of mercury amalgams permanently implanted in our teeth, chemical pesticides sprayed on our food, jet fuel that rains from our sky, pharmaceutical residue in our tap water, and mold spores that permeate our homes. So if you don't know your genetics and ignore the infiltration of toxicity into your environment and body, eventually it will become overwhelmed and some kind of symptomatology will inevitably begin to manifest, demanding your undivided attention.

The role of the immune system is to keep the invaders at bay and keep us well and alive for as long as possible. Perhaps, it's more accurate to say that it's not our immune system that turned against us, but it is we who turned against it.

TOTAL GUT BALANCE

The most important ally of your immunity is the system of digestion, as it is there that it acquires the necessary resources needed to fortify itself and become what we usually refer to as strong, and impervious to the daily assaults it must endure. It works hard to remove waste, eliminate insipient cancer cells, and build firewalls against the many viruses trying to hack into the system. When it becomes compromised, because either it is not getting enough raw resources to do its very difficult work, or it is distracted by a silent tooth infection for example, this creates a window of opportunity for the constant barrage of parasite organisms to take root.

Perhaps like the famous chocolate factory scene in the classic television show 'I Love Lucy', where my favorite redhead and her friend Ethyl calmly take each candy off the conveyor belt and place it in a wrapper. As the flow of bon-bons speeds up however, it soon becomes obvious that as more candy comes through, they start getting overwhelmed, and to the uproarious laughter of the studio audience, begin shoving the candy into their pockets, clothes, hat, and mouth, so as not to get in trouble with the humorless supervisor. So, the goal is to keep our immune system strong as we help our bodies detoxify the overwhelming onslaught of toxicity, and if you also happen to be genetically compromised, then so much more so.

As I offer my perspective on this, please keep in mind that I am simply an observer, kind of like an artist looking out into the world and trying to replicate the landscape on a canvas filtered through his own interpretation, experience, understanding, and perspective. To put structure and chart a more scientific blueprint on these observations, I invited the very best doctors in functional, biomimetic, and regenerative medicine to help either confirm my views or explain why I may be wrong. Either way, I think this will be an important conversation to have and one that will offer some insight into this world of human optimization and youthful longevity.

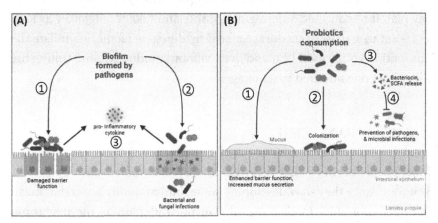

Figure: (A) Formation of biofilms by pathogenic microorganism leads to: 1) damage of the gut barrier function, 2) allow pathogens to gain access to trespass the gut wall lining causing infection, 3) leads to pro inflammatory response and cytokines release. **(B).** Consumption of probiotic and amylase blend destroy the biofilm leading to: 1) mucus formation on the gut epithelial cells, 2) colonization of the epithelial gut lining by beneficial microbes, 3) produce short-chain fatty acids (SCFAs) that support the release of anti-inflammatory cytokines, and 4) block the invasion of pathogenic microbes. These changes results in a reduction of gastrointestinal inflammatory symptoms

Speaking with a brilliant scientist with an unusual name, I asked Mahmoud Ghannoum, known as the leading microbiome researcher in the world, who spent some 40 years studying gut bugs, and recently published the bestselling *Total Gut Balance: Fix Your Microbiome Fast for Complete Digestive Wellness*, about this idea of biofilm. The revolutionary concept that bacteria and fungi weave a protective layer, an iron crochet if you will, around their hostile parasitic communities that adhere to crucial anatomical machinery and wreak havoc. In my mind it's kind of like a beehive that attaches itself to your gut lining for example. With its protective shell preventing anything to pry it off, or penetrate it, as the bugs inside proceed to poke holes in the thin layer of the mucosa, that miraculous membrane separating you from the outside world. This creates inflammation and the leaking of foreign substances into the blood stream, and that is what your immune system is fighting, and not you, as we have been made to believe. After years of research, and with the help of his son, Dr. G developed a probiotic supplement formulated as a so-called biofilm buster. I have a monthly subscription to this product and take it regularly.

And you may ask, Alex, how long do you plan to stay on this supplement? My plan it to continue ordering it monthly and take it religiously as long as I want to stay well, encourage a healthy digestive biome, assimilate the nutrients from the food I eat and live a vibrant, productive, and fulling life till at least one hundred years of age.

PREMUM NO NOCERE

Most people begin to alter their diet and become more health conscious, as it were, once they start developing some kind of health issues that make life uncomfortable. In that regard, I'm not different, as the first thing I did after being diagnosed with an autoimmune condition, and what was probably the most difficult, was to completely eliminate sugar from my diet. Some people say that this white stuff has the same effects on the pleasure centers of your mind as the other less legal and much more expensive white powder, and once addicted, reason, will-power, and self-control become futile. This was some twenty years ago, and just like the cigarettes I smoked from the age of 16 to 23, I don't give it much thought or have any cravings to want to pick up either one of those destructive habits. For some people just stopping what is causing the damage allows the body to self-heal and fully recover. For the rest of us, it will take the moving of heaven and earth, before we find our way back to homeostasis.

But find our way back we shall.

I was speaking with my virtual assistant who lives in Bogota, Columbia and who is very wise and health conscious even though she is still in her early twenties. The topic of health, and the different paradigms from where we see it, comes up often in our weekly zoom calls. One of her other clients who lives in the United States, is extremely obese. When they first met, she was taken aback as his face and neck took up most of the screen, and every so often he would pick up a two-liter bottle of soda and gulp it down for a brief eternity. So clearly for some people, whatever valve that keeps us from this kind of self-destruction, is stuck at full throttle. For my young assistant this experience was as foreign as perhaps meeting someone from another planet.

If I was to guess, the thing that is systemically damaging that proverbial valve, begins in the minds of some sinister characters who understand, that the more soda, or chips, or donuts, or cereal, or processed foods this man, and so many like him consume, the better the bottom line. Both for the six-trillion-dollar processed food, and almost five-trillion-dollar, disease management industries. And although I know that I have a predisposition to become very easily addicted to things, fortunately I also have the willpower to pry myself away from whatever that is, as I have on numerous occasions throughout my life. But I am very cognizant that even if I smoke just one cigarette today, I will be on the fast track to chain smoking and systemically poisoning my lungs and body. Hippocrates, considered the father of modern medicine, said "premum no nocere" to first do no harm, and historically this was the oath that would-be physicians took as they entered the practice of medicine.

Perhaps it would be wise for us, as individual owners of this remarkable vessel that we embody and use to navigate our life, to take a similar oath, and promise that to our own self we shall do no harm.

It can go something like this:

I swear to that mysterious and all-powerful force that brought me into this world, and one that keeps my heart beating, my eyes seeing, and my mind understanding. That spark or light that gave me my body through the love and sacrifice of my parents, for me to use however I see fit.

Shining the sun onto my face as a daily reminder of the kindness, warmth, and love that the Creator of this universe has for me. And as with any gift, it is the duty of honorable sapiens to treat it with respect and care, so that we can show our gratitude for the priceless miracle that it is.

That I am.

So then, I promise to the best of my ability to exercise regularly, provide my body with the best possible nutrition options available, allocate enough time for sleep, rest, and self-care. Make sure my vitamin D is at least 80 nanograms per milliliter, and to do no harm as I strive to live to 100 vibrant, productive, and fulfilling years.

For living fully is my way of showing sincere appreciation, for this generous gift that allows me to experience this beautiful world, in this incredible moment.

LIVER FOOD

There are a few peak performance markers that I think important and that my ScHO Practitioner and I keep track of regularly every time we do my blood work. Things like Homocysteine, Vitamin D, and testosterone vs estrogen levels, to name a few, but for my particular genetic composition, glutathione is at the top of that short list of crucially important nutrients. My friend Danielle Roberts, who I'll introduce you to in the next chapter is a Doctor of Osteopathy, and a brilliant functional medicine physician and biohacker extraordinaire, recommended that I begin supplementing with a liposomal form of glutathione that comes in liquid form. And although it's not the most delicious thing I've ever tried, primarily because of its high sulfur content, this antioxidant is responsible for, or involved in, virtually every body function that makes life possible. Glutathione is so important in fact, that it is one of the few nutrients that is actually manufactured in the liver, and when we are young it's available in abundance. As we get older, this life-supporting nutrient, as well as many others, become depleted and unless actively replenished, we experience what is known as 'extreme aging' with all the chronic conditions that come along with that phenomenon.

In her terrific ScHO Keynote that you can find on our website, Dr. Roberts goes into detail about the efficacy of glutathione and how without it the liver would shrivel up and die because of accumulations of toxins, and the body would become unable to deal with bacteria, viruses, or cancer. Once she explained the science behind this important supplement and why in my case specifically it would be a great addition to my health and longevity protocol, I started taking it regularly.

How long, you may ask, do you plan to stay on this supplement Alex? I guess as long as I wish to remain well and support my liver in its efforts to remove the toxins that may undermine my ability to live life at the peak level of health expression. So, I have it set up on monthly authorship, and consider this nutrient as a part of my grocery budget and one that I will most probably be taking for the rest of my life, or until something more effective or powerful comes along.

ITS A BUG'S LIFE

When speaking with Dr. Todd Watts, considered the 'doctor's doctor' and the 'parasite guy', who recently took in 200 million dollars in investment capital for his relatively young, but very powerful supplement line, about how he knows if his client has parasites. "There is a very simple test" he said with a straight face, "what you do is place two fingers on the jugular of the person you are treating, and if there is a pulse, chances are high that they have parasites."

We in the West have been told that these invasive organisms are only prevalent in the third world, where people eat unirradiated food, drink raw milk from an unmedicated cow, or water directly from the local stream, and don't have the EMPLOYEES MUST WASH HANDS sign in the bathrooms of their restaurants. If you've ever seen a parasite, come out of a person, it can be pretty traumatic. In the short video that Dr. Todd shared during our interview, of a young lady pulling what looked like a four-inch worm out of her nose, the stunned look on her face said it all. You don't need to be a doctor or scientist to understand how this would explain all the sinus problems she has been dealing with for years on end. And I don't know about you, but the many doctors I consulted with over the decades about my autoimmune problems, this idea of a parasite infestation, did not come up as even the slightest possibility.

One of my favorite meals when I worked at my dad's taxi shop on the west side of Manhattan in the early 1980's, was from a sausage vendor by the name of Muhammad, who had a thick mustache, and an eternal presence on the north-west corner of forty seventh street and eleventh avenue. In this particular case I had no interest in seeing how the sausage was made, as it were, but once I had such stomach cramps after lunch that my vision suddenly became blurry, and I felt like I would lose consciousness. Fortunately, after a few hours it subsided, and I went back to work giving little thought to what mysterious organisms I introduced to my body. Also, when I pulled up to the area at four am most mornings, as the night shift dropped off the cars and the day shift came in to start work, I would pick up my breakfast from the same local diner for years. As I sat at my deck in the office of the cold and empty taxi shop, I opened the blue coffee cup releasing the steam from the hot beverage, removed the cover from the disposable aluminum container revealing the over easy eggs, home fries, and sausage, and unwrapped the buttered toast. As I pulled apart the two pieces of bread, I saw a generous spread of butter, and a large, flattened water bug.

Of course, you may say that this does not apply to you, because you only eat the finest food from the finest sources and go out to the best restaurants. You only drink filtered water and always have lots of sake when eating sushi at a Japanese restaurant to kill any potential invaders that may be living in the raw fish. But sometimes when we are sold the sizzle of cleanliness, we have no idea what's behind the scenes, embedded in the proverbial steak.

There is a row of fine restaurants near where I had my shop in the west village of NYC during my late teens and early twenties. I would usually have my lunch from one particular place for years, as it was always delicious, not too expensive, and with a variety of dishes so that I would not get bored. But every so often I would try some of the other themed options that I may have been in the mood for. And there were so many. Tutta Pasta was a famous Italian place just up the block on Carmine Street, the owner used to bring his exotic car collection for service and inspections to us regularly, and it was the first time I saw the extraterrestrial Lamborghini Truck in person. Cafe Espanol was right next door, and I was friendly with the owner, Sebastian, who reminded of a Latin Humphrey Bogart and made the best seafood Paella that I ever had. French, Japanese, Greek, an authentic Italian deli, as well as Johns Pizza with an eternal line of people waiting to be seated. And a BBQ place with large neon signs of a happy pig dancing in the windows. Once, my lunch order was delivered by the elderly owner of the small local bistro. I was a bit surprised as that was not the usual choice of delivery personnel. We started chatting a little, then he said I know that you always order lunch from that other place but if you have a minute, I'd like to show you something.

We walked over to the side of the building that I would never otherwise see, and he showed me the area where scores of rats were going in and out as if it were a clip out of Pixar's Ratatouille, where a brigade of rodents took over the kitchen to prepare dinner. In no way am I saying that we need to stop going out to eat or become neurotic about the world we live in. This is just the reality, and simply because you see a 'blue A cleanliness grade' on the window of an NYC eating establishment, does not mean that the food is devoid of unwanted stowaways. There is just no way to sanitize our world so that it's completely sterile. And even if we could somehow do that, the food we eat would lose all the enzymes, nutrients, and whatever living force it has, to keep us alive and well.

WHAT'S EATING YOU

My journey into the world of cause-focused care began with a wonderful book by Dr. John AO Pagano, who wrote *Healing Psoriasis: The Natural Alternative.* In it he discussed avoiding nightshades and using teas like slippery elm bark and American Saffron to clean and repair a damaged system of digestion. Over the years John and I became friends and he spoke at many of our conferences. When the children of some of my friends had psoriasis or eczema, I would suggest they read his book and use his protocol. The results were always impressive when the client was young enough and the damage insipient. It was a little tricky trying to find all the products he recommended before the technological leap forward, but today you can easily find the entire Pagano protocol of teas, supplements, and creams, in one place just by searching his name. As his system worked to remove what was causing the damage and helped clean and heal the system of digestion it also stirred up lots of side effects. Usually, the symptoms would get worse, sometimes critically so, as people experience what's known as the 'hurx' or 'herxheimer' reaction.

We have been taught to fear and immediately start suppressing the symptoms any time our body falls into its detoxification maintenance protocols and implements a backflush. After a few months of filtering the water that comes into my house for example, our digital whole house filtration system sends the flow the other way to clean out all the filters, and then out through a center tube and on to the dirt in front of the house. This is by design and done on a scheduled basis, to keep the system from clogging up and then allowing contaminants into our drinking water.

We develop a fever, our nose starts running, we sneeze and cough, feel achy, tired, and the skin erupts like never before. This is our body's way of trying to clean itself and detoxify. Karl Herxheimer was a Dermatologist who received his doctorate in 1885 and first proposed the idea of the client reacting to a course of antibiotics to treat a particular condition, that symptoms may first become much worse, before the body begins to heal and regain homeostasis.

For me this is a great time to support my body in this detoxification process. What I usually do is water fast for a few days, try to sleep as much as I can, take a hot Epson salt bath, go into the infrared sauna, increase my supplement intake, clean out my nostrils with salt water and a drop of Oil of Oregano using a Netty pot, and just try to rest as much as possible with my eyes closed.

Fasting is probably the most powerful of the reboot and repair modalities as it allows the body to take the tremendous amount of energy necessary to digest food and focus it on doing some spring cleaning and super healing. After learning from some of the fasting centers around the world, about five years ago I decided to try and use this unusual protocol to heal my autoimmune condition. I've done different kinds of fasting approaches over the years, like a 21-day juice fast using a slow turn, masticating juicer and mountains of green vegetables. Then one where I used a medical food supplement that I would mix with some water and drink throughout the day for a few weeks straight. After hearing Patricial Bragg, the Apple Cider Vinegar heiress, author, and entrepreneur, speak at an event, about how she fasted every Monday, and did a three day fast once per month, I started a similar protocol as well. And since the lady was doing presentations and personal appearances pretty much till her passing at the age of 94, I think it's a testament to the power of this ancient modality to encourage optimal function and youthful longevity. But none of those approaches did much for me, and surprisingly, I hardly lost any weight in the process.

There are a few places around the world where people go for extended fasting retreats. On the boarder of Russia and Mongolia for example, there is a fasting center near lake Baikal said to be 25-30 million years old, that promises to improve the quality of life through calorie restriction therapy. Since the Russians did not have a thriving pharmaceutical industry, they historically relied on old fashioned folk remedies, and inexpensive approaches to help people get well.

Then there's the TrueNorth Health Center in California run by Dr. Alan Goldhamer, clinical director and founder, who has been fasting people for some forty years. They have medical doctors on staff and keep a close eye on the people who stay with them, which creates a safe environment. I learned quite a bit from some of the videos and information they have on their website. But the fellow I resonated with most was Loren Lockman, founder of the Tanglewood Wellness Center in Costa Rica. He's a bit of a wildman who fasts people for 26 days minimum and personally only eats papayas, mangos, and watermelon as his main source of nutrition. I studied his philosophy and approach for about a year, and then decided to do a ten-day water only fast just prior to a family trip. I broke the fast with a protein bar on the airplane as we were heading to Tel Aviv which sent me into such painful stomach cramps that beads of sweat appeared on my face, body, and the back of my hands. We spent about 10 days in Israel, and I ate pretty much everything they offered at the many delicious restaurants we visited, as we traveled the country from one end to the other.

As soon as we got back, I felt like perhaps the fast was not long enough, and decided to do another one, which although not originally planned to be that long, I ended up doing a water-only fast for 42 days. No coffee, tea, supplements, nothing but water from Sunday 6 pm to Sunday 6:15 pm 42 days later. Of course, I did this fast while living my life and producing a conference and journal, which is probably the worst way of doing this kind of therapy. But nevertheless, it was a tremendous learning experience to see the incredible power of the human mind and body to do what seems impossible.

The idea is that you should rest as much as you can with your eyes closed. Sleep, relax, breathe, meditate. So that all of your energy can be focused, allowing the body to do its most effective cleansing and healing. The first three days were the hardest as I experienced all the withdrawals of caffeine and food, with my stomach growling in protest. But then what happens as the body runs through all the glucose stores it switches to burning fat as its main fuel. And body weight begins to drop from 1-3 pounds per day while energy levels surge dramatically. The first ten days the mind remains hungry and throws up all the pictures of your favorite foods in full color trying to motivate you to drop the crazy exercise of self-depravation. But after that it gives up and time starts moving at a much slower pace as you need to figure out how to fill the space you allocated for the three meals, and leisurely waste removal sessions, you had every day of your life till this point.

Although I was urinating quite a bit, there was none of the other thing happening for the entire 42 days, and so the fact that I lost some 50 pounds, taking me from 180 to 130, with my body fat dropping to just 8%, was an interesting and counterintuitive phenomenon. In fact, when my mother saw me on day 35, she started sobbing since I looked like a survivor of some terrible ordeal. As the body gets into something called autophagy (self-devouring) it begins to clean and remove anything it feels could be an invader, like old cells, bacteria, and tumors. Sometime into the fifth week, I passed something that looked like a white rubber growth the size of a thumb. And other than almost fainting a few times, the experience was for the most part uneventful. My skin on the other hand, although it became less inflamed and angry during the fast, did not go through any major healing. I was quite disappointed with that to be honest. You would think that whatever was there damaging my gut would come out when it had nothing to feed on. But lucky for it, whatever it is, it had me for its continued source of nutrition.

And as long as I was still alive it was not going anywhere.

SLEEPING WITH THE ENEMIES

According to a Psychology Today article of 'Why Sleep Deprivation is Torture' by Kelly Berkley, PhD, the CIA uses this dreamy technique as part of their enhanced interrogation program to get vital information out of enemies of our nation who aim to do it harm. Usually, the individual is in a standing position with their hands shackled above their heads and is kept awake for up to 180 hours straight. If pushed to extremes eventually the subject will die because they are not able to adhere to this biological commandment. But before that happens, there are numerous stages of negative effects, starting with exhaustion, irritability, and low motivation. Then fatigue, instability, difficulty concentrating, problems with reading comprehension, inability to speak clearly, poor judgement, lower body temperature, and considerable increase in appetite. In later stages people can experience disorientation, visual misperceptions or hallucinations, apathy, severe lethargy, suicidal tendencies, and social withdrawal.

As you can imagine when we are sleep deprived, the immune system is not able to do the necessary healing. While the mind is not given the opportunity to process and attempt to make sense of everything you've thought and experienced during the day, thus creating an additional roadblock to your ability to heal and restore optimal function.

For the last thirty-five years I have been sleeping in the same room with my lovely wife, who has a very different sleep hygiene to my own. First, she does not seem to need as much sleep and is very comfortable with six or so hours to be fully rested and functional. Second, she does not like any shades on the windows and prefers to wake with the first light. Then to fall asleep, and a few times during the night, she needs to read her electronic book, that lights up the room like a streetlamp. Also, her phone is always on her night table just in case the children text, so it buzzes and lights up thought the night, and it's never the children. Then, to my objections and protests, about ten years ago she bought two dogs, a brown Labradoodle and a white Goldendoodle. Originally for each of our children, but you know how these things go. The one guy who voted vehemently against it is also the only one who ended up walking around the neighborhood placing large piles of organic matter into little plastic bags.

Both dogs, who are some forty pounds each, like to sleep in our bed, with one at her feet and the other spooning on the side. And all that is fine and lovely until one of them sees a squirrel run over the utility cables hanging from the poles in front of the large window of our bedroom, and in unison they try to remove the loadbearing wall separating them from the oblivious animal, lobbing obscenities at it in canine. Or they start licking themselves endlessly at full volume and in stereo, or they snore and twitch, scratch themselves incessantly, or decide that they want to move to my feet and spoon with me in the middle of the night.

And you may say, gee whiz Alex, why don't you just ask your loving wife and partner of many years to find some common ground, and create a more conducive sleep environment, one supportive of your health and mental wellbeing by removing all electronics, light, and animals from the bedroom? Clearly, this very good, albeit innocent question makes me think that you have never been married to a Ukrainian Warrior Princess with a slight Napoleon complex, and the negotiating style of Sergeant Hartman, the drill instructor from "Full Metal Jaket."

Now that both of my children are full on adults, and moved to Brooklyn with their significant others, an option made itself available that was never available before. As an experiment of sorts, I converted one of the smaller bedrooms into a sleep chamber that I imagined would be the most conducive for this kind of deep and restorative RAM sleep activity. It is completely blacked out, with both blinds and curtains that don't allow even a sliver of light until I open them. It's soundproof and there are no clocks, or electronics of any kind, and perhaps most importantly, I am there entirely alone.

Obviously, she did not like it and made her protest heard in no uncertain terms, but the very first night I slept for almost 14 hours. Then for the next few days, I slept for up to 12 hours at a time, leveling out at 7 to 8 hours per night, as I experienced the most vivid kind of dreams that explored and processed so many of the people and events in my recent life. Deleting tuns of data and freeing up more space in the hard drive of my mind. I felt like my brain started working faster, and I tapped that 'aether' the material that is said to fill the region of the universe beyond the terrestrial sphere. Described by Napoleon Hill in his classic book *'Think and Grow Rich'*, connecting our minds to the creativity and ideas floating in the air in the form of radio waves, texts, and black and white I Love Lucy episodes.

~

FINAL THOUGHT

"A great many people think they are thinking when they are merely rearranging their prejudices." – William James

Chapter 9

MEDICAL MATRIX

You can't solve a problem in a system that profits from its existence.

From the moment Neo takes his first gasp of freedom, in the iconic scene when the matrix, a complex system that has been sucking his life energy to power the machine, while providing him the bare minimum to keep his body alive, begins its relentless attack aimed at his destruction. Up until that moment our hero was living his best life, albeit in a coma, doing all the things we're told will make us happy and fulfilled. Yet somehow, he knew, somewhere in the deep recesses of his subconscious mind, that something was not right.

He did not fit in.

Most of us who are awake enough to know of its existence, and courageous (or reckless) enough to speak our minds when attacked, always have a little doubt in the back of our mind, like dew on morning grass. It makes us question that perhaps it is "I" who is crazy. How could it be that the system we were born into, the one we spent our entire life trusting and serving, could sell us on a well-coordinated world-wide scam, and force us to shut our businesses, mask our children, entomb our families, and donate our bodies to science under duress?

All the while telling us to "trust the science."

Danielle Roberts, DO

In the real world, when the matrix is threatened, it can quickly, and with little thought, attack and destroy those it considers a danger to its own survival, simply through the process of accusation. It can bring to bear all its authoritative might. Using the three branches of evil, namely corrupt enforcement, treasonous politicians, and promiscuous media.

If we are to reform this matrix, we will never be able to do it with people it works to enrich, but only with those it tried to destroy.

Imagine for a moment, that you spent your entire life becoming a physician. Right from the start you noticed a sense of deja vu, the black cat and the glitches. Frustration incited by a system set up to manage endless effects, turns into outrage when what was disguised as ignorance, finally reveals itself as intentional extortion, when those running the system attempt to force vaccination on all medical staff. At that moment you, along with a few other student physicians, decide to go protest this government enforced vaccine mandate.

Eventually you realize that you are just a cog in a huge multi-trillion-dollar behemoth that focuses all of its energy on the management of well-established disease but has little interest in understanding the underlying cause. Placing the mighty dollar above those you swore an oath to protect and serve and heal, while increasing relentless demands on your time and mind to the point of exhaustion and burnout. By the time you understand that you will not be helping people stay well and avoid the heavily traveled road to most modern disease, as you may have envisioned, it is too late.

Now, you're trapped.

You spent enough of your youthful years sacrificing your personal life, and much of your family's money, getting into a system that looks very different from the outside than it does within the depth of its dark and cacophonous underbelly. At this point you realize that there's no way out. Either you surrender your soul and try to go through the daily rituals, simply going along to get along, or you find a nice quiet place and empty a bottle of sleeping pills in your mouth.

As suicide is a pandemic within the ranks of these remarkable people. Making the medical doctor number one in self-termination among all other career choices.

The other option is that you try to educate yourself on all the missing pieces necessary for you to be able to practice medicine on your own terms and outside the all-seeing matrix ... outside the hospital system, the 'health' insurance bureaucracy, and governmental social schemes. So, you attend every self-development course you can find. Those that can hopefully help you become a more rounded healer, like nutrition, personal training, IV therapy, and reiki to name a few. At the same time, you'll need to learn everything you can about leadership, sales, communication, and business skills - subjects conspicuously lacking in the very expensive medical education.

And this is where her story begins...

I've known Danielle Roberts since around 2008, when she first came to some of the wellness walks, we organized to promote the Science of Human Optimization conferences that my team and I produced. At the time she was still in residency with this idealistic plan to wrestle health care away from the powers that be and create a more sensible and proactive model. Once she received her medical degree, she spoke at some of our ScHO events on engaging the power of the subconscious mind in the healing process, including concepts such as the placebo effect.[1]

Full disclosure, I like Danielle. She is one of the kindest, most authentic, and brilliant doctors I've had the pleasure of working with over the years. She is honest to a fault and righteous beyond comprehension, with neither carrot nor stick able to get her to compromise her integrity. When you know someone for that long, it is very difficult to believe when dubious groups you've come to look at with disdain come throwing disparaging accusations, as if it was a biblical stoning.

In this chapter I invited Dr. Roberts to explore the deficiency and toxicity that contributes to most every scourge we are dealing with as a society, but before we do that, I'd like for you to get an insider's peak at the tools in the system wielded to destroy her life and reputation. Perhaps with some grace, a little luck, a whole lot of skill, hard work and courage she can build a new life outside of the matrix and help bring truth and healing to the masses.

Let freedom ring.

By Danielle Roberts, DO

IRON LADY

Alberta is a remarkable single mom, nearly super-human intuitive air traffic controller, who became a client. She's now 67 years young and a grandmother.

Who thought she was dying.

The pain, stiffness, and swelling started in both hips, "I can't put my socks on now – I have to have my son help me." Both knees were inflamed. Her right shoulder flared more than her left and was "working its way down my arm to my wrist and hand. I can't brush my teeth. I can't put on my bra ..." She was waking up often during the night in pain, needing to use the bathroom, but couldn't get out of bed to make her way there. This all happened suddenly, within a three-week period. Throughout her life she has experienced episodes with joint pain and swelling but never this bad. I can see why the conventional doctors she saw thought that her persisting joint pain was infectious by nature.

Alberta went to a primary care provider, who landed on Post Streptococcal Arthritis, gave antibiotics (Bactrim) for seven days, and diclofenac, as an anti-inflammatory, for fifteen days. The urgent care doctor she visited ordered lab tests that revealed high liver functions (or liver damage) and sent her for an Ultrasound. Hepatitis and other causes of liver dysfunction were ruled out.

But what were they missing?

If it is "an infection" causing the inflammation in her joints (and now liver), what allowed for it to take root? It turns out Alberta's ferritin, an iron-storage protein in the blood, was high. Iron is necessary for our red blood cells (hemoglobin) to carry oxygen to all our cells, so that they can make energy, but can also be toxic if absorbed in elevated amounts. This was a routine medical diagnosis of hemochromatosis, a disorder where an individual is born with a genetic blueprint guiding their intestines to absorb iron from their food in abnormally elevated amounts. Unfortunately, both the urgent care doctor and the primary care doctor missed this.

Perhaps, because they were looking at the problem from the disease management paradigm.

Alberta started a "hemochromatosis diet" which is low in iron (mostly vegetarian since animal meat is rich in blood and therefore iron). She made sure not to combine iron containing foods with vitamin C which increases its absorption, but rather with calcium (dairy) which blocks the absorption of iron. Additionally, she started supplement binders, and nutritional support that allowed her body to eliminate (or detoxify) the excess iron (and other heavy metals) from her system.

Her pain decreased significantly in just a couple of weeks. She started sleeping through the night, she began walking again, going up and down stairs, and getting to the bathroom easily. She was able to put on her own pants and clothes. She could brush her hair, and teeth, and was back to caring for her grandkids and their home. Most importantly she was able to make her family's RV excursion from Alabama, all around Massachusetts and back, when just a few short weeks prior the lack of mobility and pain prevented her from attending her mother's funeral.

This is a nutritional toxicity and deficiency issue.

But where does it come from? In this case Alberta's absorption process was influenced by her genetics, but with a proactive, cause-focused approach, we were able to help her tweak her environment to better steer her genetics and body in the direction of the optimal function and homeostasis.

THE MATRIX GLITCHES

In 2008, at the age of 26, I was a third year Family Practice Resident at NSLIJ Plainview Hospital, being mandated to submit to the Flu Vaccine. One that is used to prevent a virus. However, I held a contrarian view of virus'—I didn't believe they were necessarily something we need to, or should prevent, based on my direct experience of children who had milestone breakthroughs when they were allowed to overcome febrile illnesses without medications. The human genome project sequencing revealed 43% of our DNA is in fact viral particles, confirming my understanding of toxicity and vitality, and annual circadian rhythms. I believed the virus might exist to help us detoxify and evolve to better interact with our environment from one year to the next. Also, this virus is not life-threatening (unless in elderly, chronically ill, or the immunocompromised).

Also, the company that was offering the vaccine did not provide long term studies, while some of the ingredients (thimerosal, formaldehyde, polysorbate 80, MSG) were documented to be linked to Alzheimer's, infertility, and the like. Needless to say, I did not have enough information to want to inject this substance into my body.

I was prepared to leave residency, medicine, and everything I had worked for up to that moment. I flew to Washington to march with others against this mandate and talk to our representatives. While there, I attended a four-day international vaccine conference held by the National Vaccine Information Center. It became even more evident that the science wasn't clear. Pharmaceutical companies were refusing to do long term or twin studies on the vaccines they were mandating our children take to attend school, and subversively sticking them as soon as they are born as a matter of routine care, i.e. – the Hepatitis C vaccine which is irrelevant to newborns as they are clearly not sexually active.

These were not well thought out recommendations.

It also became clear that the science behind the efficacy was shaky. The CDC graphs of declining disease around vaccine implementation were skewed to attribute declining deaths to vaccination programs. When in fact 85% of the disease decline took place prior to WWII (c. 1940), a period where few antibiotics, modern medicines, or vaccines were implemented. Diphtheria, tetanus, and pertussis for example, became available during the late 1920's but were only widely used in routine pediatric practice after WWII. Making it impossible, or very doubtful, for them to be responsible for the impressive declines in mortality seen in the first half of the century. Declines were more likely attributable to clean water and effective sewer systems.[2]

Some information from clinical trials, was just blatantly being withheld from the public or distorted, like the increasing incidence of shingles in the elderly when the varicella vaccine was implemented. And this wasn't the only area of medicine where this was happening.

What was going on here?

The matrix was glitching more and more often as I pressed forward in my pursuit to understand what was keeping our country helpless and sick.

Fortunately, they finally dropped the forceful directive at that time (2008) – however, this was just a premonition of what was to come in 2020. Needless to say, I completed my residency program, became a licensed physician, and continued my quest to help empower people to live lives they love, while maintaining my autonomy to choose what is injected into my body.

The full scope of the matrix, and the underpinnings that have created it, would come into full focus for me over the next 15 years as I continued my quest to change the face of medicine.

DEFICIENCY

Alberta has just one of the about 129 million diagnosed chronic health issues American's struggle with.[3] – not counting those we aren't aware of or just think are "normal." I believe 95% of all chronic diseases are preventable; caused by our daily choices and lifestyle habits.[4] Many are traceable to nutritional deficiencies and toxic overload, and relatively easy and economical to correct. It's kind of sacrilege at this point in medical evolution that these things would not be preventatively evaluated annually.

So, what is deficiency?

Simply, according to The American Heritage® Dictionary of the English Language, "it is a lack or shortage of something essential for health." If the cell doesn't have oxygen, it can't make energy and dies, correct? It is deficient in oxygen.

There are 13 essential vitamins.

Vitamin A (retinoids and carotene), Thiamin (B1), Riboflavin (B2), Niacin (B3), Pantothenic Acid (B5), Pyridoxine (B6), Cobalamin (B12), Biotin, Ascorbic Acid (vitamin C), Choline, Calciferol (vitamin D - prohormone), Alpha-Tocopherol (vitamin E), Folic Acid/folate/folacin (B9), and phylloquinone/menadione (vitamin K).

There are 16 Essential Minerals.

Calcium, chloride, chromium, copper, fluoride, iodine, iron, magnesium, manganese, molybdenum, phosphorus, potassium, selenium, sodium, sulfur, and zinc. Amino acids, organic acids, and fatty acids (omega 3, 6, 9) are also noteworthy.

If the cell is deficient in these nutrients, it will, at the very least be impaired and age rapidly, at worst, it will die. So, what causes these deficiencies? To answer this question, we have to look at every step in the processes of digestion, absorption, and circulation that our physiology books so nicely lay out.

Let's start with our food.

Where does it come from? Where was it grown? Is the soil depleted of vital minerals and nutrients or light energy? Is it sprayed with pesticides (which add toxicity and decrease phytochemicals)? Is it processed after being harvested? If not, is it fresh when it gets to you or have the nutrients started to break down and degrade? What happens in food processing? Are nutrients bleached, stripped, heated and destroyed, pasteurized, homogenized? Are there any nutrients left by the time it gets to you in the store, fast food chain, or restaurant?

If there are, do you cook it?

What cooking process do you use? Are there nutrients and aliveness in your food when you eat it? How do you eat it? Is your nervous system and digestive system ready to digest, meaning are they relaxed and ready to secrete the proper enzymes and hormones? Are you in fight or flight, or rest and digest? Do you chew? How well? Do you secrete proper saliva, stomach acid, enzymes, bile? Do you have a good robust microbiome (bacteria balance in your intestines)? Is your gut inflamed and not absorbing nutrients efficiently? Do the nutrients you're eating impede each other's absorption? (i.e. calcium blocks iron absorption, while vitamin C increases it). Food modernization (more accurately, the matrix) has made eating very convenient, but nourishing ourselves, very inconvenient.

If you could improve any one of these things, it would have a positive impact.

Many of these issues can be addressed by improving the freshness, wholeness, and quality of your food, as well as your process of eating; simply breathing, being grateful, and chewing. However, there are a few vital nutrients that you must pay particular attention to because they are very difficult to get within our current food system in the United States. In addition, if you have mistreated or neglected your gut for years, it may also benefit from some TLC (detoxification, biofilm dismantling, leaky gut damming, and candida cleansing), so that it can actually absorb the nutrition from what you are feeding it.

Iodine:

Some 97% of Americans are deficient in this essential nutrient. Every cell needs iodine. Many people know it is essential for thyroid function, but you need it to make every hormone in your body. Iodine levels in the US population have fallen 50% over the last forty years. There was an explosion of glandular issues and cancer during that time.[5] I've supplemented myself and my patients for years when I was practicing, to help them prevent thyroid disorders and hormonal issues. I caught a lot of flak at that time as many practitioners were afraid to precipitate an episode of thyroid storm.

However, only five to seven people per one million, in the United States experience thyroid storm, and most are not caused by a gradual increase in iodine. Individuals with goiter or other preexisting thyroid issues that were injected with a large amount of iodine containing contrast were typically at risk, not those that mindfully start supplementation and titrate up.[6] Having a practitioner who can monitor your optimization program is always a plus. In Japan they eat about 13 mg of iodine a day safely and have much lower incidence of thyroid disease and glandular cancers (i.e. - breast, thyroid, and prostate).[7]

Simply and cheaply, I use Lugol's solution 13 mg of 3-6 drops per day. This bottle will last about a year. So, for an investment of $15 dollars annually, you can potentially save hundreds of thousands of dollars in medical cancer care, time off from work, suffering, pain, and impacted loved ones, while experiencing a higher quality of life.

Quite the bargain.

Vitamin D:

Your skin makes this versatile pre-hormone when it is exposed to a pinking dose of sunlight. How much vitamin D you make depends on your age, how much skin is uncovered, and your skin tone. Without sunblock and with arms and legs exposed, your skin will make 10,000 to 15,000 units of vitamin D in one pinking sun exposure, on average. (Sunblock, with an SPF of more than 15, blocks 100% of vitamin D production in the skin).[8] Deficiency prevalence data is somewhat inconsistent because the definition of 'deficient' is inconsistent in this case. There's a 60-70% prevalence in the United States according to the Endocrine Society definition of <30 nanograms per milliliter. The 2011/2012 National Health & Nutrition Examination Survey (NHANES) asserts that 41.6% were insufficient.

More importantly, here are the risks and benefits associated with specific levels of vitamin D:

<15 ng/mL: Severe Deficiency–increased risk of rickets.

<20 ng/mL: Severe Deficiency–75% greater risk of colon cancer.

<30 ng/mL: Deficient–increased risk of depression and seasonal affective disorder, bone loss, poor wound healing, muscle pain, joint pain, diabetes, schizophrenia, migraines, autoimmune diseases, allergies, preeclampsia, and inflammation.

30-50 ng/mL: Suboptimal Levels–twice the risk of heart attack, increased incidence of high blood pressure, and three times the risk of multiple sclerosis (MS).

50-80 ng/mL: Optimal Levels–50% reduction in risk for breast cancer, decreased risk of all solid cancers, slower cancer growth.

100 ng/mL: Excessive–increased risk of toxicity symptoms due to elevated blood calcium levels.

Depending on where you live (your latitude), you may only get enough UVB radiation from the sun for vitamin D production between May and October. Also, the darker your skin, the more sun you need to make enough vitamin D. However, sunlight is essential for more than just vitamin D – but I'll leave that to Dr. Joshua Rosenthal, a quantum medicine physician, to explain in Chapter 10.

Your genetic make-up can also impact your body's ability to absorb and utilize nutrients. We now have the technology to identify our genome and particular genetic expressions, or polymorphisms that may contribute to personal issues you may have metabolizing certain nutrients. Celiac disease, MTHFR, and hemochromatosis are just a few that you can readily check for, that can lead to deficiency and toxicity, cell damage, disease, and premature death.

Folic Acid:

Folate or folic acid is essential for the body to make DNA and RNA and metabolize amino acids necessary for cell division and maturation of blood cells. Without this our cells don't divide or replicate. Individuals (such as myself) may be born with a polymorphism for MTHFR.

Simply put, if you have this gene, your body has a much harder time using the folic acid you take in to help the cells function. The conveyor belt backs up at stage three, leaving a mess and no finished product. For us individuals the solution is simple ... take in 5-MTHF folate, instead of folic acid, or possibly just additional folic acid. If your B12, or homocysteine levels are high, this is a good clue you may want to consider genetic testing and supplementation. Such a simple change can prevent neurological defects in your children, spontaneous abortions, dementia, cancers, heart disease, and so much more.[9]

Glutathione:

Selenium, Vitamin C, and cysteine are needed for glutathione (GSH) production. Glutathione is the most essential antioxidant in the body. It is made by our liver but can become deficient with age (particularly after 40) and with inclining toxic exposures or burdens. This effects every cell in our body and is associated with EVERY disease or dysfunction known to man.[10]

Simply put; low GSH, high disease and shorter life. High GSH, lower disease and longer life.

As well as having too little of a vitamin or mineral, we can also have too much – there is a "just right" spot necessary for life. As we learned in Alberta's case, the Iron Lady, her iron absorption was not in the sweet spot, but rather toxic.

TOXICITY

Back to the cell: If we want to live longer and better, our cells need to live longer and better... so what are the effects of toxicity on a cell? They are virtually identical to that of deficiency; dysfunction, mutation, apoptosis (death), and poor communication. Our bodies are equipped to eliminate toxins well and regularly. We have five pathways that our body uses to eliminate waste. However, over the past two decades, deaths caused by pollution have increased by 66%. Industrialization, uncontrolled urbanization, population growth, fossil fuel combustion, and an absence of adequate national or international chemical policy are likely primary contributors to these deaths. Toxic exposure causes more than nine million deaths each year globally.[11]

This number has not changed from 2015 – 2022.

In addition, we are exposed to toxins earlier in life (EWG detected an average of 200 out of 287 chemicals in the umbilical cord blood of our babies in 2005. Had they tested for more chemicals they likely would have identified more). In addition, we are depleted of the nutrients we need to detoxify properly because of the quality and processing of our food. Likely leading to the rise in disease we are seeing in our county, including autism (10X 1980-1996), leukemia (62% 1973-1999), asthma (2X 1982-1993), and childhood brain cancer (40% 1973- 1994).[12]

In a 2015 epidemiological systematic review found a 19.1 net percentage increase in incidence and prevalence of autoimmune disease per year in the past three decades. This rise was attributed to the influence of environmental factors, more heavily than genetic ones, and these increases correspond with environmental toxic load exposure in individuals living in industrialized countries.[13]

Studies with twin subjects have found that an environmental trigger is necessary to turn on the genetic expression of these diseases, and that genetics can only account for increased susceptibility to autoimmune disease. All this points to environmental chemicals as a significant factor in the development of autoimmunity in susceptible individuals.[13]

What is a toxin?

The Merriam-Webster dictionary states: "A poisonous substance that is a specific product of the metabolic activities of a living organism and is usually very unstable, notably toxic when introduced into the tissues, and typically capable of inducing antibody formation."

However, even water can be toxic – yes, I've treated patients with water toxicity. But is water a poison? No ... and yes. The reality is life requires a delicate balance. The cells in our body require a pH of about 7.34 give or take some mild shifts, similarly it requires a delicate balance of Na+ (sodium), K+ (potassium), Ca+ (calcium) and many other ions (minerals) to allow our nerves to communicate through the electrical signals they send. If those signals become disrupted in the heart, for example, no more beaty beat.

No more life.

Luckily our body is magnificently and intelligently made and if our kidneys are working well, they filter our blood, measuring our water and ion levels and reabsorbing what we need while letting go of what we don't. However, they can be "overwhelmed", and our water levels can "dilute" the minerals we need to sustain life. Certainly, water serves an important purpose and is VERY necessary for life – poisons and toxins are not. There is a train of thought that stressing the body with toxins occasionally, to strengthen or fortify it is a good thing, perhaps to shock it back into action if it's clogged, sluggish, or complacent (kind of like getting into a cold shower when your body is suffering or complacent) – however, on the regular, our current postindustrial environment offers too much toxicity, and our typical Americanized daily habits and substandard nutrition are not equipping our bodies to handle it.

Toxins to consider: persistent organic pollutants (pesticides, herbicides, organophosphates) toxic metals (mercury, lead, cadmium, arsenic), solvents, endocrine disruptors, drugs, chlorine, forever chemicals (PFAS). These are now ubiquitous in our food, drinking water, household products, and even in the air we breathe.

As discussed previously, toxic environmental chemicals induce several physiological mechanisms that lead to autoimmunity. Toxic chemicals can also induce epigenetic expressions of DNA, which leads to autoimmune disease. Lastly, toxic chemicals deplete antioxidants such as glutathione and promote immune dysregulation and deterioration of immune barriers; including the blood-brain barrier, the intestinal barrier, and the pulmonary epithelial barrier, in the lungs. The combination of these physiological alterations, together with genotypes that have polymorphisms in immune regulatory regions, leads to autoimmune reactivity or autoimmune disease development – and this is just one type of disease process (endnote 13). We are not discussing cancer, or other chronic diseases primarily contributed to by chronic inflammation, such as heart disease, strokes, diabetes, or the like. But suffice it to say, if wear and tear is happening in your immune cells or throughout your immune system, it is likely happening in all your other cells as well - they are one and the same. Everything is connected. Remember, most cells need the same things to survive, and they are vulnerable to the same poisons.

There are accounts where people have been exposed to toxic substances and lived, were even unaffected, or became strengthened. I postulate that these cases have something to do with our belief systems or perhaps different genetic polymorphisms and environmental circumstances. Others are necessary for life but become toxic when out of balance: water, iron, fat soluble vitamins, sugar, caffeine, food, and most other biological substances.

Inputs to be aware of and minimize:

These are toxic sources we're exposed to regularly, but have some control over: large predator fish consumption, pots, pans, dishes, food storage containers, unfiltered tap water, skin care products, in house air quality, foods (pesticides, herbicides), mercury fillings, arsenic and lead in untested supplements like protein powders, rancid oils (from frying, or restaurants that reuse oils to fry foods), and rancid coffee beans (to avoid this, grind immediately before use, or don't use). EWG.org is a great starter resource!

Outputs to maximize: The 5 systems that provide waste elimination:

The digestive system is the pathway of cells from the mouth to the anus. In addition to digestion and assimilation, it consolidates our waste and eliminates it. If the gut is leaky the waste does not get eliminated. It leaks across the mucosal lining into the blood creating double duty (pun intended) for the liver and other organs, i.e. - leaky gut). Normal elimination is 1-3 effortless bowel movements a day. I'll say that again ... 1-3 effortless bowel movements a day. Of course, fasting or other changes may affect this, but I've had patients that would report going once a month!

This is NOT normal and very taxing on the body.

The Urinary system: The kidneys filter our blood, and excrete excess ions, water, urea, and waste into our ureters, which are tubes that connect to our bladder. The urine is stored there, until we can excrete it. Water typically helps us "flush" our system (water toxicity is very rare and often happens in the elderly or those with dementia that wind up with a compulsion to drink). Still, consider not drinking distilled water or reverse osmosis water without mineralizing it first. Dehydration (along with certain bacteria, and high oxalate foods) can lead to kidney stones. Proper hydration can help prevent this painful condition as well as help our bodies expel unwanted toxins.

The Skin: Our largest organ sweats out water and minerals but also many toxins that our body wants to eject. Dry brushing and Rebounder exercise can stimulate our lymphatics and improve circulation to the skin, and therefore waste removal.

The Respiratory System: Exhale. Yes, do that again! Our lungs expel CO_2 (carbon dioxide) which is an acidic waste product in our bodies. If someone comes into the emergency room metabolically acidotic (acidic - i.e., with a low pH – yes, this is the same measure used in swimming pools) the first thing we do is put them on a ventilator and increase their breathing rate to "breath off" the excess acid and bring them back to metabolic balance compatible with life for their cells.

Breathing also highly regulates your nervous system. If you're often in a stressed state your body releases cortisol, and adrenaline often. This inhibits detoxification in all the pathways listed here. It also adds to oxidizing the body and creates toxic byproducts that age our cells more quickly. Oxidation in the body is chemically identical to the rusting of an abandoned car.

Go ahead ... take another deep breath, it's free!

The liver is the fifth way our body helps us neutralize and eliminate waste, and it is the only one that doesn't have a direct pathway out of the body. The liver acts as a sieve to filter our blood of all toxic metabolites, to neutralize and ready them for elimination through one of the other pathways. There are four phases of detox aptly named; Phase 1: Phase 2: Phase 3: Phase 4. If phase four is blocked (if you're constipated), your body has a negative feedback system set up to shut down the process at Phase 2 so that the body doesn't create more toxic metabolites that can't be eliminated.

If you are going to start "pushing" your pathways to try and speed up the detoxification process, there are ways to open and prepare your body for drainage and release of toxins. So that you don't release them into the bloodstream without providing a way out of the body. If you do, these toxins that your body had intelligently sequestered away into your tissues, are now floating throughout your system and wreaking havoc on the other cells. This increases cellular turnover, shortening your cell telomere length, along with your lifespan.

Without doing more elaborate detoxes that may be risky without experienced oversight, you can start to support and open these pathways. I have created an entire course that teaches how to optimize these functions, but here are a few simple tips that can improve your bowel movements, urination, sweating, breathing, and liver function.

Simple ... not always easy.

SIXTEEN STEPS TO DETOXIFICATION AND OPTIMIZATION

1. Start breathing: do you catch yourself holding your breath often. Let go. Breathe. Regulate your nervous system to stay in "rest and digest" (the parasympathetic mode of your nervous system). It is in this gear only that your body can let go and detox, and this is also the only gear in which your body can digest and assimilate nutrients. So, in addition to getting rid of acids and helping your pH stay balanced, it sets the foundation for all the other systems to be able to do their job well and nourish and cleanse your cells.

Happy cells, happy life!

2. Stay in "rest and digest": Your stress response, "fight or flight" is meant for EMERGENCIES. For many of us this means eliminating (or decreasing significantly) our coffee intake, and other stressors to help your body stay in rest and digest. Practicing good emotional hygiene is imperative; take time to intentionally relax; walk in nature, meditate, make love, go dancing, practice yoga, try painting ... do whatever works for you.

3. Give thanks, especially before you eat: Besides the amazing perceptual benefits of gratitude, it actually improves your heart rate variability and therefore decreases all-cause mortality (check out Heart Math). In addition, it helps your body switch out of fight or flight and gets you back into "rest, digest, detox, repair, and flow state".

4. Chew your food, experience your body taking it in, breaking it down, and becoming satiated.

5. Stop eating just before you're full. Don't overwhelm your digestive system, as it will clog up the pipes and decrease your body's efficiency to deliver nutrients properly and eliminate waste.

6. MAKE TIME to poop! We can tell our body other things are more important, and literally, not give it permission to go. It's important, prioritize it.

7. Small meals four times a day work well for many – there are no rules here. Find what works for you. Incorporate fasting or intermittent fasting from time to time to build character, self-restraint, and allow for bowel rest and cellular recovery (see Fast Like a Girl).

8. Choose whole, unprocessed foods. If you don't recognize what's listed on the ingredient list, don't put it in your body. Keep processing to a minimum.

9. STAY hydrated! Obviously, this helps your kidneys and urinary elimination, but it also assures that you can have those 1-3 effortless bowel movements a day.

10. Get in the sunlight. Vitamin D is not the only reason. See Chapter 10 and quantum theory.

11. Do not eat after sundown. Most of your repair and regeneration is done while you sleep. Your circadian rhythm regulates all of your hormones and cellular heath signals in this process. Insulin spikes from eating late inhibit the hormones (i.e. – growth hormone) that repair your body overnight and alter cyclical signals. In addition, digesting overnight steals energy from our regenerative process in order to digest. This is counterproductive. Stop it!

12. Magnesium: If you are still not pooping well. Natural Calm or Mary Ruth's nighttime mineral blend are two of my favorites, if you're having a "hard time" (pun intended). Remember 1-3 effortless bowel movements a day (unless you are fasting).

13. Sweat! All the time. Stop using the AC, lol

14. Exercise: it is the fountain of youth, and one of the only ways to naturally stimulate your body to make and release its own stem cells.

15. Take inventory of all the toxins you encounter on a regular basis, i.e. in your daily routine; what you wash with, brush your teeth with, moisturize with, deodorize with, cook with, clean with, and eat. The water you drink

and bathe in, the air you breathe, the EMFs you expose yourself to, and medications you use. Eliminate the major sources of toxins you expose yourself to daily to decrease the burden on your body and liver.

16. See a Science of Human Optimization practitioner. Get your nutrient levels, and preventive markers checked annually. Supplement the nutrients you are low in, especially the ones I mentioned earlier in this chapter. Maybe, learn one new thing about your body annually: test your microbiome, your genetic polymorphisms, and your heavy metal burden.

Invest in your body.

It is the only one you will get, and the only place you have to live, for the rest of your life!

This is a very basic understanding of the structure and function of our bodies. Ultimately if our cells can't make energy we die. These concepts are not difficult or complex. In fact, what it takes to get and keep a body healthy and optimally well is fairly simple (especially if we start early and teach our children through our own example). However, in a society that would like us to remain sick and dependent, it becomes exceedingly more difficult to implement the basic lifestyle habits that allow our bodies to thrive.

BRANDED FOR LIFE

I am far from perfect.

In fact, if perfect is way over there, then I'm way over here, inconspicuously wiping lipstick from my teeth. As I painfully witnessed so much unnecessary suffering and death at the hands of our current system of indefinite management of chronic disease, I was pursuing knowledge through every possible course and education program I could find. The last and most ambitious one caused me a bit more trouble than the others, but also made the real problem crystal clear. If only I did what they wanted. If only I sold out the people I love and trust and played the game by the rules of the men and women with loud voices, and badges and guns and self-serving agendas.

I could have been "enriched" instead of summarily destroyed.

They tried to break me, but instead my soul was tempered, my vision cleared, and my heart purified. Through this process, I learned that I was impervious to their threats and bribes. I was willing to be tied to the stake and burned alive, before I would bear false witness, for some silver coins.

This is a story which I am currently working on, and one that will ultimately fill a few volumes. In light of the adversity, attacks, and destruction, my life's mission is clearer than ever, and my resolve annealed. I will use all my knowledge, passion, and creativity to bring forth the resolution of unnecessary chronic illness for our nation, expose and resist injustice, and protect truth, science, and humanity.

$\approx$

FINAL THOUGHT

"The day the power of love overrules the love of power,
the world will know peace."– Mahatma Gandhi

Chapter 10

LIGHT AND SLEEP

On the cutting edge of science and technology the human
potential for self-regeneration is both miraculous and mundane.

by Joshua Rosenthal, MD

How does one find the holy grail of youthful longevity?

As a sleep doctor, it seemed to make sense to start with what was right in
front of me. Ask someone how they sleep, and you have a fifty-fifty chance
they will say, "pretty good". This was the same answer I had gotten from
patients with very severe Obstructive Sleep Apnea, a disease that causes
them to stop breathing many times per night and lose oxygen in their
bodies. Maybe human beings aren't good judges of a state of being where
they are literally unconscious. It would make sense evolutionarily that
we would suppress knowing about our sleep deprivation. Running from
a predator with the knowledge that we had a terrible night's sleep might
dissuade us from trying hard to survive.

So much is said about the importance of sleep, but no one really seems to
know how to get this daily regenerative therapy running optimally. The
textbooks talk about the basics and what can go wrong, but it was clear
that the list of "sleep hygiene" given out to all those with poor sleep, hasn't
produced positive results. This seemed to me the place to start figuring
out the secrets of optimal health. Create a strong foundation with the

Joshua Rosenthal, MD

mysterious nighttime journey we spend a third of our lives doing, and maybe you'd be on to something.

For the specialty of sleep medicine, it's honestly a bit "cookie cutter". Said patient comes in with sleep complaint. Said patient gets ordered a sleep test. Said sleep physician reads sleep test results to patient. Done. Many will end up with a diagnosis like Obstructive Sleep Apnea or even lesser-known diagnoses like Periodic Limb Movements of Sleep, but many also will be told everything is "normal". I always felt very disappointed to tell someone they had a normal sleep test when it was clear that they didn't sleep well and had daytime consequences of that poor sleep. After every patient like this, I felt the need to carefully review the many pages of tables and graphs of sleep data, looking for a common denominator, the missing piece for obtaining quality, restorative slumber.

DREAMING OF BETTER HEALTH

It might have been a few hundred tests, or it might have been a thousand, but at some point, I felt I found a trend. Those with poor sleep and "normal" sleep tests, didn't really have normal tests at all. The stages of normal progress through a slightly repetitive sequence of light sleep to deep sleep, to light sleep again, then to dream sleep, and back again to light sleep. This pattern repeats with most deep sleep in the first half of the night, and most of the dream sleep in the second half of the night. These stages have huge connections to our physical, psychological, and emotional health. Dream sleep is known to improve cognition, memory consolidation, emotional processing and overall brain wellness. Deep sleep offers great physical body benefits such as hormonal release and detoxification of the brain (known as the glymphatic system). After my analysis, there were abnormalities in the sleep architecture, the stages of sleep, in all these "normal" people. Results either had a deficiency of deep sleep, dream sleep, or both, and sometimes the problem in the architecture appeared to be a fragmentation, essentially a bumpy ride with a very herky-jerky back and forth transition between the stages.

Why shouldn't the sleep stages be optimized, and how would one do this?

The scientific method starts with a question which then develops to prove or disprove an answer to that question. It seemed appropriate to start my own citizen science project in search of the secrets of great sleep. Therefore, I strapped on a consumer level EEG brain wave recording headband every night and studied my sleep. Each night I tried different supplements and techniques to see how it would affect my own sleep stages in hopes of finding the Rosetta Stone of sleep optimization. Would taking a precursor amino acid to melatonin improve my sleep? How did different vitamins and minerals change my sleep architecture? Was there some nutritional adjustment that could cause my sleep to be better or worse? This was a fun time of experimenting, trying to manipulate only one of many variables at a time that could change the quality of my slumber. While I did not accomplish this very ambitious task to create the exact formula for perfect sleep, I did learn many things about my physiology and started to ask even better questions.

What truly was the most important controller of sleep to get right?

Every sleep physician has read a chapter on circadian rhythms and the biochemical/genetic control mechanisms. The chapter in every textbook is the same, showing a fancy biochemical teeter-totter that helps to tell time in a cell, allowing night and day to be distinguished. It would seem to the reader that this is just a chemical reaction which goes on and on like any clock or watch. However, the human clock system runs slightly longer than the single 24-hour daily cycle. In this way, if it was left without daily synching, it would slowly fall out of time until the day seemed to be night. This free running clock system is seen in some people with blindness, who will fall in and out of true time slowly because of the lack of the clock being reset each day. The disease is called non-24-hour sleep-wake disorder, and it is a malfunction in the clock mechanisms of the eye and brain to tell time properly. People with this condition gradually find their bedtime and wake time advancing from minutes to hours each day until they will actually wake during night and sleep during the day.

This continues over and over again, finding a short period of being in synch with the clock and gradually running away from that synch. This brings us to the textbook description of what sets this clock, "zeitgeibers". These are the very things that wind and set the clock, literally translated "time givers". There was no mention of exactly how the light system worked in these chapters, however, there usually was talk of bright light therapy when trying to avoid jet lag from time zone changes. It was clear that precise timing of light could certainly adapt the circadian clock system forward or backward when used properly. It was never discussed in the setting of optimizing sleep without needing to change the time zone.

SLEEP APNEA, MIGRAINES, AND VITAMIN D

It was at this time that serendipity struck me. The absolute truth is that I was online watching a video when the sidebar video recommendations caught my eye, "Sleep apnea, Migraines, and Vitamin D". As a professional, I had no idea how these three things went together, so I felt the need to click and find out. This video led to an hour-long lecture about how Vitamin D was not really a vitamin and was more like a hormone, both migraines and sleep apnea had a similar controlling area in the brainstem, there were Vitamin D receptor in this area, and treating with high dose Vitamin D to get appropriate serum levels would make many people's sleep and headaches normalize.

Having never heard such a thing about Vitamin D and having mostly only seen subpar levels when this was tested in the blood, I was curious to find out more. So naturally, I tested myself, first getting my 25-hydroxy-Vitamin D level optimized to over 60 ng/mL, I felt more energy and better vitality overall. Next, I took it to patients. And some, not all, would literally start to sleep better instantly. There were no adverse side effects other than my Endocrine colleagues not being so happy with this new protocol that they were certainly unfamiliar with. This was a crucial piece of the puzzle, for sure, but since it couldn't help everyone, there had to be more to the story.

At that time in my life, I was focusing on my own nutrition more carefully. It was evident that wellness had to be the sum total of all the small choices you make on a daily basis. The better the choices, the better your health.

The quarter of a million-dollar medical education I paid for provided me with many textbooks on disease, and maybe a few sentences on wellness. Intuitively, I knew that every day was a domino of health leading toward another domino. Stacking the wrong choices together led to disease.

Stacking the right choices together led to longevity.

But what were the right choices? The dogma of the day continues to be "diet and exercise". However, in both my personal and professional career, that was obviously a fallacy. With new diet and exercise books coming out monthly, the obesity crisis seemed undented. I had patients tell me they were adversely gaining weight whilst working out in the gym. If everyone was using the technique of diet and exercise to achieve wellness, why were there so many failures? Could it be that we were missing something? Again, my interest in nutrition had led me down a more "Paleo" dietary template. This was based on paleolithic man's access to food and what he would choose as the basis of his diet. This eliminated most of the processed foods, and left only natural, properly grown sources of whole fruits, vegetables, and meats. I would always think, "what would a cavemen eat?" to facilitate my culinary choices away from packaged, instant meals, to simpler whole food choices.

The truth is that when I graduated from my residency program, I was tipping the scales at 220 pounds. I had had enough, and promised myself that now as a new attending physician I would regain a healthy physical appearance. The only answer I had was "diet and exercise". In trying to keep balance between my professional life and personal life, I crunched the numbers to figure out the most efficient way to do this. Science says that 3,500 calories equate to one pound of fat loss. If I did high intensity workouts for one hour a day (which would equate to about 500 calories burned), seven days a week, I would be able to lose one pound per week. That seemed like a poor return on investment to me, seven hours of hard work to lose only one pound. Instead, I downloaded an app on my phone and proceeded to eat 500 calories less per day instead. This required me to learn a lot about weights and measures, but because of my intense discipline, after 3 months I was eating 1000 calories a day and had lost 50 pounds.

The only problem was I looked terrible!

My face was gaunt, and it looked like I had just gotten out of the hospital for some serious illness. This required regaining about 15 pounds to fill in and "appear" healthy. It didn't make entire sense back then that I could look unhealthy after losing 50 pounds, but this would be one of the better questions that would come back to me just as I was learning about Vitamin D and trying to better understand the secrets hidden in sleep for optimal health and youthful longevity.

SEEING THE LIGHT

So, large amounts of Vitamin D3 were able to drastically improve people's headaches, and sleep problems, but "what would a caveman do?" This same solution to eating better types of food, begged the question, how did cavemen improve their Vitamin D levels. They certainly couldn't eat enough fish to get to the type of levels that supplements were replacing. It was obvious that they must have been getting it the way humans evolved to get it, through ultraviolet light. They spent way more time outdoors in natural light and way less time indoors under artificial light. Just wearing clothes blocks the frequencies and energy of the sun from being absorbed, compared to the way our ancestors lived with skin in the game. This was directly opposite of the environment of those whose labs showed low vitamin D levels. And it was at this moment that I saw the connection between this dietary problem and the sleep problem that I was so curious to solve.

It was light.

It had always been light. Its very nature was why it was so obvious yet so hidden. It is right in front of you, but you don't necessarily appreciate it for what it is. You certainly don't realize the difference in light frequencies present when you walk from inside to outside as being significant. This realization turned my world upside down, in the best of ways and in the worst of ways. Light is not governed by biochemistry. Ask a physician about physics and expect to hear a lot of silence. If light-controlled vitamin D production and light controlled the circadian rhythm, there must be physics involved before any of the biochemical processes that I learned in medical school can occur. Light works with electrons and protons, and it is on this small quantum level that health must first start. The Human Genome Project did not deliver on the promise to eradicate many of the diseases we're currently dealing with. Because we now understand that, in fact, what really matters is how the environment affects genes, a field called epigenetics. Therefore, the environment was the smoking gun for manifesting disease. This explains how known centenarians (those living past 100 years of age) could have the breast cancer gene (BRCA), but never develop breast cancer or ovarian cancers. Up until this point in my life, I had only considered toxic chemicals as the environmental poisons to avoid. I now realized that light was an important environmental factor that I had not considered or knew enough about.

BACK TO THE BOOKS

If light can control the biochemistry of the human clock, then it is necessary to understand how the biophysics of light operates to find optimal health. There are many scattered resources that are needed to see how all this ties together. One of the earliest books I found which explains a lot about light is John Ott's, "Light and Health". Ott is well known for the time lapse photography of flowers blooming. His book documents his journey to understand light and the effect it has upon living organisms. He encountered difficulties when he took flowers into his studio to photograph, which turned him onto the fact that not all "light" is the same.

He found that the frequencies of light which came from the artificial light sources changed the way living organisms behaved, stopping rare flowers from blooming and changing the sex of offspring of mammals. The frequencies of the sunlight contain all colors of the rainbow, while artificial bulbs have subtracted much of that spectrum to become efficient. These frequency deficiencies are a cause of epigenetic changes that impact the behavior of living things. Ott even developed a light bulb which had much less absent light frequencies that improved the overall wellbeing of those who used it. His book details many vignettes which explain the power of light on plants and animals. It is a worthy read for curious individuals. This book did not explain the actual quantum mechanics of light's touch on organisms but did shed "light" on where I needed to look to find the secrets to longevity.

As I re-learned physics and began to develop a grasp of quantum physics, it became obvious that this was all an energy story. "Hue-mans" are in fact, beings of light. This is not new information. Many of the studies of light and how it impacts life are over 50-75 years old in the published literature. A great number of publications were being made in Russia, which limited much of the growth of the field in the Americas due to a language barrier. However, much of it has been translated, summarized and published by Roeland Van Wijk *"Light in Shaping Life: Biophotons in Biology and Medicine"*. In understanding how cells use light to run the biochemical symphonies, one can start to understand that humans are not much different than the smart phone technology everyone uses. Wireless information traveling invisibly through the air converts to information that can be displayed on a screen, into sounds that can be conveyed across the globe, and can be transformed in various ways that seem almost magical. When realizing that everything must be energy and information that is used to optimize human function, it becomes clear that there must be an organizing gear of this machinery.

When I investigated the gory details of how this worked, it became obvious, where it all pointed to.

QUANTUM ENGINES

We all know in medicine that we have electricity running through our bodies. An electrocardiogram, EKG, and electroencephalogram, EEG, are diagnostic tests that every physician is familiar with. However, when you start asking a doctor about how this electromagnetic system works, they will likely answer with a metaphor of wires connected to a pump or computer. This simplistic view grossly underestimates just how wise mother nature was in designing human physiology electromagnetically. Humans are able to harness every aspect of the physics of light, electrons, and protons to their advantage. Light is in fact nonlinear, which is quite different than the "one plus one equals two" linear world we are generally familiar with. This principle allows one plus one to equal one thousand. It is the butterfly effect. Truly, a small flap of a wing in one place, can cause a hurricane in another. To create optimal health and longevity, we need to strive for optimal bioenergetics in our cells.

When this is done properly, amazing accomplishments of regeneration are possible, such as a young child completely regenerating the tip of a finger.

Unlike a salamander who can completely regenerate an entire limb at any time, after about age nine this human fingertip regenerative ability is lost. Human body bioenergetics are entirely too complex and energy depleting to maintain this vestige of regeneration that much simpler organisms kept. However, this should inspire hope that an approach to health with biophysics holds the secrets of longevity and regeneration when applied.

To begin this quantum biophysical dance, we must first look to where the energy and information is processed in the cells. And where do we create time and energy in our cells? It turns out that the answer lies in mitochondria, the powerhouse of the cell, which has been underestimated and only taught to medical students as the machine that makes a cellular currency of energy called adenosine triphosphate, ATP.

Gilbert Ling helped to show with very complicated mathematics that the amount of ATP produced in cells was horribly less than what was required to run a cell. The medical community was not aware that this discovery was shattering to the chemical ATP energy paradigm that is still used today. The Nobel Prize for Chemistry was given to Peter Mitchell for his chemiosmotic theory of energy in the cell. This belief, despite Ling's dismembering with mathematics, has persisted in the scientific and medical community for decades. Unfortunately, cells are utilizing much more complex light and sound based energetic and information-based communication that is rarely utilized in the standards of healthcare that exist. Mitochondria literally holds the power to keep us optimized, as well as innovate and create the solutions to our health problems. In the mitochondria, we maintain timing mechanisms of when to produce different biochemicals, create energy in multiple ways to run these systems, and transform environmental signals into instructions that will allow us to thrive in current situations of existence.

Douglas Wallace at the University of Pennsylvania has discovered the details of mitochondrial function and bioenergetics. His published studies show that broken mitochondria lead to disease, and that replacement of these deficient mitochondrial engines eliminates disease. This finding should have changed the face of medicine, shifting the paradigm to Mitochondrial Medicine as the new future for studies. While studies are expanding, this focus has yet to materialize. With this knowledge, no disease should seem unfixable, because when the mitochondrial function is restored, in many instances, the disease disappears.

This all started to connect to sleep when I found out that mitochondria make melatonin in the cell when exposed to infrared light. This is not the pool of melatonin that is often spoken of at night as helping us fall asleep. It turns out melatonin is also a powerful antioxidant of the brain, a helper to lower high estrogen, has anticancer properties, and facilitates repair of mitochondria allowing regeneration. Mitochondria produce free radicals from electromagnetic environmental signals which are in fact instructions for the cell on how best to optimize biochemical functioning to survive in that environment. They have been most studied for their response to making free energy from red and infrared light frequencies. It should not come as a surprise that these are the most heavily subtracted light frequencies from our cost-saving light bulbs. Furthermore, it should also be no surprise that the frequency found most in these popular light bulbs is also the most damaging to the bioenergetic and circadian clock systems we use.

DIET AND EXERCISE … AND LIGHT

When I realized that the artificial light frequencies were hurting my health and sleep, it was time to do more citizen science to understand how to stop the damage. While I was still learning the gears of these systems,

I purchased a cheap orange pair of goggles that could be worn over my prescription glasses at night when I was working on my laptop finishing electronic health records. What used to leave me tired and wired when I closed the computer for sleep, and resulted in feeling slightly groggy in the morning, suddenly changed to yawning and quality sleep. I would now wake the next morning feeling fully refreshed and ready to conquer the day. So, I continued with wearing these blue light blocking glasses while on the computer regularly. At this time, I was eating a Paleo template diet, and my weight was stable. Additionally, I was so busy as a new physician in practice and as a husband and father, there was no time left over for exercise. Three months into this new blue blocking practice, I happened onto the scale and noticed a seven-pound weight loss. This was especially surprising since the only change I had made was light based. I decided to recheck an annual blood panel, and to my further surprise my fasting blood glucose was lower, my markers of inflammation were lower, and my testosterone was significantly increased. These findings would correlate to the science I was soon to discover on the underlying mechanisms of light on circadian and mitochondrial function.

If putting a filter over my glasses could impact my entire physiology, how much more wellness was being left on the table because of biophysics?

Turns out that light frequencies through the eye control neuroendocrine function. Allowing the right light can improve your mood, your hormones, and your metabolism. Epigenetic environmental switches are being turned on by the frequencies your environment communicates to your cells. Controlling these gene variants to optimize physiology for the environment you are in is the task of light and the electromagnetic spectrum. Living in the north pole, and living on the equator, requires different types of advantages to survive. Evolution selected the mitochondria to adapt to these differing energetic situations. More than 35 years ago, Douglas C. Wallace, PhD, showed that there are mitochondrial variations based on human evolution across the globe. These haplotypes, the subtle variations of mitochondrial fuel processing, allow more efficient use of the environmental light signals to modulate metabolic function for survival. If someone changes the signals that are received, they can completely change their destiny. Therefore, epigenetics claims that you are not predestined for your family's diabetes or heart disease. While you may adopt the same routines that create the signals, you have the ability to change them and change your health. This is very empowering for those interested in optimal health and youthful longevity. Learning how to change your electromagnetic environment, from the artificially created indoor signals to more natural outdoor-like signals, can make a huge impact.

MOVING TO QUANTUM HEALTH

After realizing that small changes can lead to huge health impacts, it is very exciting to learn more. Basing therapies on repairing mitochondrial health can improve overall bioenergetics and allow disease reversal. This explains trends in red light therapy, intermittent fasting, and cold-water immersion therapy. Anything that improves mitochondria will be directed at changing general health. Once I had my lab results from three months of blue blocking glasses, I doubled down on biophysical therapies. Adding cold therapy to my regimen allowed me to lose the weight I had previously gained to look healthy. This time, at my fittest weight, I looked trim as if I had been working out regularly. Quantum health is all about bioenergetics, mitochondria, and circadian timing. Proper energy at the right time can turn back the chronologic clock, allow regeneration, and make all the systems that a human needs to thrive, work better. This became my top priority personal and professional focus, repairing the damage done working 100 hours a week, with little to no sleep from my medical training.

Utilizing these techniques and protocols, I was well on my way to changing my own health as well as my patients. To understand the difficulties faced in healing, we must understand the dynamics of mitochondrial function. The fact is that mitochondrial function decreases about ten percent for every decade lived. This means it is an uphill battle for everyone to reverse the poor health they are fighting against. Aging is the ultimate mitochondrial toxin that seems unavoidable. However, technologies exist that can restore function back to youthful vitality much more rapidly. These regenerative techniques often involve intravenous therapies of light, photosensitizers, mitochondrial stimulants, oxidative therapies or stem cells. Special light absorbing compounds can be injected prior to light therapy which will enhance absorption and delivery of the energy to specific areas of the body.

In this way, you can target weakened areas with the right types of energy that will repair and restore function. Oxidative therapies can help eliminate chronic infections, help the body detoxify bioaccumulated chemicals and metals which interfere with function, and reduce inflammation. Finally, the most powerful treatments involve using cells which have strong energetic stores and the ability to create a whole new human being; stem cells which were the original cells that built you from scratch at the very start of it all.

SEEDS OF CREATION

There is much interest in umbilical cord blood banking. This tissue contains embryonic stem cells and compounds that support the production of all the organs and all the connections necessary at birth. It is unclear whether unfreezing cells and using them much later in life is the way in which we should approach this. How to best use these cells later in life after a human being has already been created is somewhat unknown. It seems reasonable that using these cells to rebuild deficient organs in some way is the recipe for true healing. Whether thawed or already alive in your body, stem cells hold the keys to fixing that which is failing. An ideal therapy for regeneration of any faulty system would be minimally invasive, perfectly matched to one's DNA, and targeted to damaged areas.

This technology is not one for a science fiction movie, as it already exists today. There are known embryonic-like stem cells, VSELs, which are floating dormant around in your blood as you read this. Once activated, these may in fact be nature's "cord blood bank" for extreme conditions. When taken from their dormant state to an activated one, they can do what they were designed to do and that is to create any component of your body. Such VSELs are pluripotent, meaning they can make almost any kind of cell type that is required in your body. Should a cardiac cell need to be repaired, they can make it. Should a brain neuron tract need to be revitalized, they can perform this. Should a kidney or liver cell need rejuvenating, they are able to do that as well. This is nature's way of 3D printing a new organ inside of your body using your own DNA, and your own building blocks, no new machine needed at all.

This is the ultimate regenerative technology.

Most of us have heard of stem cell technologies used to repair damaged joints. Typically, these procedures are using Mesenchymal stem cells from fat or bone marrow. These stem cells are quite large and can't travel through the blood freely and require some sort of injection to achieve delivery to the target. However, we know that these types of stem cells are specific and are only able to make a small number of cell types. Additionally, these cells age and lose their potency over time making them less able to repair damaged tissue as we age. They also require a more invasive harvesting by drilling into the bone to obtain marrow or performing a liposuction to obtain stem cells from fat.

VSELs, on the other hand, have the advantage of being in your blood, so procuring these cells is only as invasive as placing an intravenous catheter in a vein, no different than any IV. Since they are so small, they can traverse your entire blood vessel system and cross the blood brain barrier giving them access to your entire brain and spinal cord without cutting through your skull or placing a special catheter into your spine.

VSEL technology has been shown to significantly decrease biologic age when examined with the latest biochemical blood tests. This means that advanced aging can be reversed, and there have been publications using such techniques that have shown improvement in heart failure patients who were candidates for heart transplants. Having a minimally invasive technique that improves heart pumping function after it has been damaged without the need for continued immune suppressing medications changes everything. Now diseases can be thought of as the sum of their broken parts. Parts that can be repaired and replaced with better functioning versions made with the unique DNA that they were designed to have.

This means that a stroke with nonfunctioning brain tissue could be repaired with the exact same neurons and the exact same blueprint from birth. These technologies are still in their infancy, but the ability to interact with diseased organs and systems can be performed with little risk or downside. It is only the amount of repair and locations of the downed systems that need addressing. The future of medicine is bright when one looks at it through the lens of regenerative medicine. Previously diseased tissues of any age may now be refreshed.

It isn't science fiction anymore.

LIMITATIONS, NO MORE

Using a paradigm of bioenergetics, longevity and anti-aging therapies will slowly gain popularity. Allowing a human body to restore the proper timing and regain energetic function starts off the type of health reversals that have only been pipe dreams in the past. Harnessing the power and energy of a single cell is how nature creates a perfectly functioning human, no drugs or interventions required. This is the technology that will bring an end to human disease and restore wellness. By first rebuilding the circadian mechanism, the body can unlock the timing mechanisms required to start slowly regenerating in the artificial world we live in. Then, when needed, more powerful rejuvenation can be used to fill the deficits that years of poor epigenetic choices have created. We are all able to achieve the health we want, one micro decision at a time.

The choice is yours.

~

FINAL THOUGHT

"If you want to find the secrets of the universe, think in terms of energy, frequency, and vibration." - Nikola Tesla

Chapter 11

ORAL HEALTH & LONGER LIFE

It may be true that all disease begins in the gut, and
it's also true, that all guts begin in the mouth.

By Jimmy Kilimitzoglou, DDS

"Hi, I'm Jimmy Kilimitzoglou" I said to a visibly frightened patient by the name of Doris, who was looking up at me as she nervously fidgeted in the dental chair. Her response to my innocent greeting was a brutally honest and authentically visceral "I hate you!" This was my fourth year of dental school, and although somewhat unpleasant to hear, I certainly understood what she meant.

My most challenging patient, who successfully avoided visiting the dentist for some thirty years, also happened to be my father. Working as dental lab technician for decades he also did not like or trust dentists. Having witnessed the inner workings of this mysterious group of doctors, he only half-jokingly referred to them as butchers. So, by the time he found his way to my dental chair, he had a severe case of periodontal disease. As a heavy, lifelong smoker there was advanced accumulation of tartar, plaque, and debris, the gums as well were inflamed, and many of the teeth loose.

Complicating matters, he had what can only be called a severe dental phobia.

Jimmy Kilimitzoglou, DDS

When I explained that we would have to do multiple non-surgical periodontal therapies as well as some alternative treatments. He said he would follow my lead. "I will try anything to save my teeth" is how he put it. That is exactly what he did. This strong, proud, and confident man, who was terrified of dentists, put his trust in me, his son. Little by little we saw small improvements, less bleeding, less tooth mobility, and less inflammation.

Using biological treatments, minor short term pharmacological intervention, laser therapy, and advanced, customized oral hygiene protocols, my goal was to first stabilize the damage and then work to reverse it. Doing a salivary analysis, genetic testing and bacterial culture, revealed that although his risk for periodontal disease was high, because the anaerobic bacteria were abundantly populated, he was at a very low risk for cavities. I used this information to custom-tailor his treatment. Modifying the bacteria with the use of certain probiotics, we balanced his oral micro-biome. Applying low dose medication to clean and disinfect the deep, hard-to-reach pockets between his teeth and gums.

In time, the results were nothing short of a miracle.

Any other dentist would have either abandoned him, or simply took the simpler and better reimbursed option, and performed a full mouth extraction. After managing his phobia, listening to his concerns, and expectations, I came up with a plan. We worked together using the least invasive, most natural, and effective therapies and materials, allowing my father to keep his teeth for the rest of his life. Over the decades since, I've worked with countless patients just like him. Some less challenging, while others even more complex.

They are all uniquely rewarding.

MY LIFE'S PURPOSE

When I was six years old, growing up in Athens, my unlikely superhero was also my dentist. I was truly mesmerized by the high-tech equipment that surrounded us, as if we were in the cockpit of a jet liner. He was meticulous, methodical, confident, and borderline arrogant, with his dexterity and skill. Press a button here water squirts into a cup over there. Press a button there, a light turns on overhead. The man also had x-ray vision, with the help of a futuristic camera, that was able to see inside the human body. Peering through skin, muscle, ligaments, and bone. Everything was clean, and sterile, and welcoming. His shiny instruments found their way, dancing around my teeth, tickling my gums.

I never felt any discomfort.

Each visit inspired and intrigued me to look forward to the next checkup. At the dinner table I asked my mom and dad "does a dentist make a good living?" They both smiled and chuckled, quietly nodding yes. Ever since my dream has been to one day become a dentist. For me it's more than a job, occupation, or career. For me it's a calling. It's my life's purpose.

GD put me here to take care of people and use my hands to comfort and heal.

After residency, my first experience was working in a bustling office that accepted every form of dental insurance, and provided services based on the agreements set forth by the individual group. The patients were of a low socioeconomic background and simply went along with the procedure that their insurance covered, and that the office was willing to perform. As the client came in, we would take x-rays and collect pertinent data, submit it to the insurance company for preauthorization and present the results to the patient.

If the insurance company approved a root canal, post, and crown, we would be able to save the tooth. If, on the other hand, they deemed the tooth unrestorable, we would perform an extraction. It gets worse. If the administrator (not a dentist) submitted for a root canal, post, and crown, even though the tooth did not need major intervention. And if the insurance company gave us the go-ahead, we would present this over-the-top treatment option to the patient, who usually consented, and we subsequently performed the procedure.

185

I questioned this directive, saying "but the tooth can be treated with a large filling or crown. It does not need the root canal." The response I received is "oh, this insurance plan is lenient, and they usually approve the root canal, so that is what we're going to do." Take it a step further, some of these insurance plans would cover x-rays every six months. Again, I questioned this perverse incentive, "but this particular patient has a low risk for cavities and does not require x-rays every six months" I reasoned. "It's ok, this insurance covers it and pays for the (dubious and redundant) diagnostic." Wink. Wink. Went the tacit reply.

The patient's autonomy was nonexistent. My schedule there was inhumane. In the six-hour shift, they would book thirty patients for me to see. The treatments were not simple: root canals, impacted wisdom teeth, orthodontics, fillings, and crowns.

The breakneck pace, creating a perfect environment prone to errors, oversight, and omissions.

Insurance has impractical and rigid rules. There are alternative benefits for which they downgrade treatments. For example, if there are eight contact points of teeth or less, they will cover partial dentures. If there are more than eight contact teeth, they feel that you have enough teeth to chew. So, if you happen to be missing your front two teeth, the insurance company won't pay for replacements. If you need a filling for a molar, they will not pay for a tooth-colored option, but an amalgam with high mercury content. Instead of a porcelain crown, they will pay for a cheaper, all-metal one.

Often, they would pay for an extraction, rather than saving a tooth, because obviously it will cost them less. If you have a crown or denture that is damaged or is failing, they will not pay for it if it is less than ten years old. What if you accidentally bit into an olive pit and the crown broke? Sorry, you must wait until that ten-year mark. They will pay for antibiotics, but not probiotic therapy, which is more beneficial, natural, and does not have adverse reactions, listed in long disclaimers following pharmaceutical advertisements. There are non-covered services that you can benefit from, but it doesn't fit their business model or help their bottom line. In most states there is legislature that mandates insurance companies use at least eighty percent of their revenue towards patient care.

Of course, New York State has no such law.

There was one insurance company that only used thirty percent of their revenue toward health care. Let's face it, these people are in the business of making as much money as possible, and not trying to solve your health problems. They don't care about your overall health or wellbeing. They don't care about toxicity in cheap materials, nutrient depletion, the health of the oral biome, supplementation, detoxification, laser biostimulation, or advanced, biological, and personalized high-tech care.

Their ikigai, or reason for being, is profit.

But in practical terms, there is just no way to provide exceptional, sophisticated, integrated care in a modern, caring, boutique setting, with the finest materials, and high-tech equipment, along with a dedicated team of customer-care professionals, at the unreasonably low insurance reimbursement rates. The menu pricing has to represent the quality of the materials, resources, expertise, as well as the vehicle with which they are delivered. In a free-market model, the fee schedule is carefully crafted to provide great value for the high-quality service and be sustainable.

Heavily insurance-based practice, on the other hand, is notorious for a revolving door of staff, assistants, hygienists, and even dentists. The appointments are brief, and the services are often rushed so that profitability is maintained. You cannot pay a hygienist fifty dollars per hour, for example, and then spend an hour doing a thorough cleaning, when the insurance reimbursement is forty-seven dollars and fifty cents.

Losing money on every client, while trying to make it up in volume, is not a great business plan.

The rule is that a hygienist needs to produce three times their salary to cover the overhead. Therefore, they will get less than twenty minutes to execute the cleaning, performed on fast-forward, and in a hurried, callous manner. If we accept the below-market, third-party payment for that service, and then allocate the full hour to the client, while using the highest quality materials, with exceptional, highly paid personnel, the practice will shut its doors within a year.

It is simply not sustainable.

The phrase "you get what you pay for" applies remarkably well. But you really should only pay for what you need when you need it. If you don't need x-rays every 6 months, you should not have to submit to unnecessary radiation, or pay for the scans automatically. Same goes for root canals or any other procedure driven by perverse incentives.

My dream practice was a niche of integrated oral care with a "less is more" driving philosophy. That one-stop-shop of high-quality dental care that I mentioned earlier. I wanted to model it after a high-end boutique hotel crossed with the technologically advanced Tesla factory. Catering to phobic and holistic-minded patients who had total body health, and youthful longevity in mind. Well-meaning colleagues told me things I had to do to succeed. "You can't set up where there are a lot of dentists. You have to accept some insurance plans. You need to see as many people as possible and do as many complicated procedures as you can. If insurance does not cover it, patients won't pay out of pocket."

Turns out none of that is true.

Driven by the belief that "if you built it, they will come" I was willing to risk everything to bring this distant vision to reality. High tech, high touch, high end, and minimally invasive oral care. People are happy and impressed with the service, the welcoming office space, they love our staff, and inevitably refer their family and friends.

Success naturally follows.

Miners brought canaries into the coal mine, because it had an accurate, yet sometimes sad way of predicting disaster. The mouth has a similar ability to predict a person's overall wellbeing, not only to detect a preventable catastrophe early, but as the beginning of the digestive process, it can help us fine tune things to provide optimal function. From inflammation, biome, and acidity level to bone integrity, immune function, and even brain health.

Your mouth is the first place to look for cause-focused healing.

The one body part that gets the most medical intervention over our lifetime, from drillings, root canals, and extractions, to fillings, injections, and surgery. Is also the last place where we look for the cause of our subsequent health problems. In fact, before one of our functional oncologists considers taking on a case, they first send the potential client to a biomimetic dentist. Where the three-dimensional cone-beam scanner is used to check for a silent tooth infection that maybe diverting the attention of the immune system away from where it's needed most.

Killing cancer cells.

MERCURY FILLINGS

A good example, and the main difference between biological "biomimetic" dentistry and traditional kind, is their approach to mercury amalgam fillings. A high percentage of treatments for oral conditions and diseases use toxic materials. Often patients have old amalgams defacing their beautiful pearly hills of the natural tooth structures. Studies suggest that some people can be sensitive to the mercury contained in those active metal fillings. Patients with mercury toxicity have experienced irritability, brain fog, headaches, fatigue, and early onset Alzheimer's disease.

As most people know, mercury is a heavy metal that can be detrimental to the central nervous and immune systems. Amalgam, a commonly used filling, has more than 50% mercury. Once removed from your head, the dental office must use very strict EPA directed hazardous waste protocols, to dispose of this neurotoxin. According to new research, most Americans are exposed to more mercury from dental amalgam fillings exceeding the safety limit.

Dental procedures like gum cleanings and root canals, can release mercury vapors trapped in the amalgam filling, forcing bacteria and heavy metals into the bloodstream. In ominous proximity to the brain. To minimize this risk, holistic biological dentists often use natural antibacterial agents during the procedure. We also partner with functional medicine doctors, like those mentioned in this book, to support the whole body through this optimization process. Our goal is to make sure that the liver's four phases of detoxification are being properly supported, and that there is no bottle neck in the process that will cause a backup of toxins, resulting in more damage or stress on the body.

Using supplements like chlorella before, during, and after the mercury filling extractions, is just one small example of this.

SILENT TOOTH INFECTION

Did you know that oral infections up-regulate several systemic inflammatory reactions that, in turn, play a role in the development of systemic diseases? Multiple studies around the world have investigated the association between oral health and autoimmune diseases. Experts have concluded that poor oral health significantly exacerbates the incidence of chronic health problems. How can modern, minimally invasive, biomimetic dentistry identify and resolve oral infections that may be contributing to the cause of these conditions?

Healthy gums are supposed to be coral pink in color because they are highly vascularized with hundreds of fine blood vessels. In fact, if you unravel the gums that intimately hug our teeth, the part of gums that you cannot see visibly would be the same size as the palm of your hand. If you measure the surface area of all gum tissue, lining of the cheeks, tongue, palate and floor of the mouth it would amount to the area of your entire arm. Once compromised with gingivitis or periodontitis, inflammation can move quickly throughout the body like a raging forest fire. Thus, resulting in mini strokes, coronary heart disease, as well as premature, and low birth weight babies.

With a direct correlation to poor blood sugar control in diabetics.

Because of this highly vascularized nature of the mouth, bacteria get into the bloodstream faster. Think about this. If someone is having chest pain or a heart attack, where do we place the nitroglycerin tablets? That's right, under the tongue. It dissolves quickly and gets into the bloodstream virtually instantaneously. Bacteria and toxins can enter the bloodstream just as fast. The mouth is the first portal into our digestive system. But indirectly, you can see how it can become a portal to the circulatory and respiratory system as well.

There are autoimmune diseases that have oral manifestations such as Lyme, psoriasis, irritable bowel syndrome, skin blistering, and arthritis. Patients with periodontal disease create immune cells that are inflammation biased. As this cycle continues, there is progressive tissue breakdown and diminished repair capacity. Gum tissue is frequently challenged by bacterial biofilms and are subjected to this phenomenon. As periodontitis progresses, these elevated pro-inflammatory mediators and cytokines produce insulin resistance, contributing to systemic disease.

This is how periodontitis can trigger and exacerbate diabetes.

Periodontal disease affects one out of four diabetic patients. Poor blood glucose control increases the risk of gum disease and vice versa. Diabetics who are not well controlled are more prone to poor wound healing, higher risk of infection, problems tasting food and less salivary flow. This makes them more susceptible to cavities, as well as inflamed and bleeding gums. It is a vicious cycle, and patients end up with loose teeth, mouth sores, bad breath, white patches, and a sticky, dry feeling in the mouth.

There is a strong link between periodontitis and Crohn's disease. When people have uncontrolled periodontitis, they have inflammation that travels throughout the system of digestion. This exacerbates gastrointestinal issues in a patient with Crohn's resulting in flare ups. Inversely, Crohn's disease interferes with normal absorption of nutrients, and patients don't get enough calcium or vitamin D to maintain normal bone health. This translates into continued bone loss and gum tissue degeneration in the mouth. Nutrient deficiency makes periodontal disease worse because of collagen breakdown and biome imbalance.

MISSING TEETH MISSING YEARS

When we chew our favorite meal, the teeth come together and slide between each other, the peaks and valleys (or cusps and fossa) break down the food. The more time we spend chewing slowly and deliberately, the better we prepare the nutrients for assimilation. This allows preliminary enzymes to initiate the digestive process. The healthy bacteria in our mouth, or oral biome, also contribute to early digestion. Improperly or inattentively chewing food can lead to indigestion, as large food particles enter the stomach only partially broken down. This can create cramping, gastrointestinal issues and unwanted weight gain.

So, what happens if someone has no teeth?

What about the elderly who have lost all their teeth and have no dentures? There are conditions like periodontitis, or genetic disorders where people are born without teeth, and indigenous people in parts of the world who intentionally extract teeth for cultural reasons.

Many of them become susceptible to obesity because it is easier to eat soft foods high in carbs and fat.

In anthropology we study the past and examine skulls of ancient man to learn more about ourselves as a species. When you look at cavemen, they ended up having 32 teeth, perfectly straight, never having braces, never having crowding, never having sleep apnea. As a matter of fact, crowding was never noted until about 500 to 600 years ago. The people that did have crowding were nobility. The aristocrats who could afford softer, fancier foods ended up not stimulating their jaws, teeth, ligaments, and muscles of the mouth. The result was crowding and crooked teeth. Turns out that hard foods started at an early age stimulate the lips, cheeks, tongue, and teeth in a way that allows for proper growth and development and perfect harmony leading to straight teeth. The foods that were available in the earlier days were of hard consistency and it promoted exercise of the oral musculature. Like any muscle in the body the principle of use it or lose it applies. Therefore, if the lips and tongues are not stimulated, they end up atrophying. That means we lose strength and tone in those muscle groups that are not properly stimulated.

The healthy pressure of hard foods allows proper tension and resistance of muscles, increase blood flow to those muscles joints as well as bones and ligaments. Hyperactive lips and tongue results in extruded teeth. This crowding discourages growth and development of the jaws and does not allow for permanent teeth to come into the mouth and set properly. When we feed infants a completely liquid to soft diet we don't help them with their oral musculature. Conversely, we encourage weaker muscles for chewing and swallowing. Hundreds of years ago babies would gnaw on ribs, beef jerky, berries, nuts and vegetables without ever choking or having abnormal jaw development. The tongue, pharyngeal constrictor muscles, cheeks and lips were accustomed to the tough consistency of the food that was available to them. If we introduce children to these types of foods, we will improve their future development.

When the teeth, jaws, muscles and joints are in perfect harmony it is the ultimate level of oral optimization; a true, well-oiled machine. If one thing is off balance, the whole system is compromised.

About 180 million adult Americans are missing at least one tooth and the overwhelming majority have many missing teeth. More than 35 million of our citizens lost all of their teeth, and ten percent of them cannot wear dentures, and must go around completely toothless.

Missing a front tooth may be emotionally dreadful but missing even one back tooth creates silent havoc on your overall health. As the number of missing teeth increase, so do diseases, inexplicable weight gain, and risk of death. Here are just a few of the recent scientific findings. "Tooth loss increases your risk of stroke and heart attack, both deadly. Tooth loss also increases your risk of rheumatoid arthritis. If you are missing five or more teeth your chance of pancreatic cancer increases by twenty percent.

And people without teeth live ten years less than those who can hold on to their pearly whites.

The reasons for these associations are both obvious and yet undiscovered. If you think about it, digestion begins in the mouth. It is no surprise then, that improperly chewed food has a devastating and far-reaching impact on our health. Food that is not properly chewed may not be fully processed, robbing your body of vital nutrition. According to the latest peer reviewed research, poor nutrition, combined with increased stress on the body leads to diseases, suffering, misery, and early death.

In view of this information, it seems obvious that preserving your natural teeth (with the "less is more" protocol) for your entire life should be one of our primary pursuits. Along the lines of eating healthy, exercising, getting enough rest, and being positive and optimistic. Sadly, the odds are against us. Today our teeth must survive longer than at any time in human history, simply because we are living longer. This trend will continue, especially within the health-conscious community, like the readers of this book. Primitive dental carpentry, during the years of the Wild West, worked when life expectancy was about forty.

Perhaps, these outdated techniques, once performed by the local barber, are not the most optimal choice today, as we are living into our nineties, and beyond!

ORAL BIOME

We have more microorganisms on us and in us than we have our own human cells. The symbiotic relationship is vital for our health and well-being, at the same time, we are host to a myriad of bacteria, fungi, and viruses. It is a well-balanced ecosystem like a large aquarium or a lake. When things are balanced, every organism thrives in harmony. However, if there is a disruption of that balance, it throws off our healthy microbiome turning the pristine lake into a putrid swamp, leading to chronic symptoms and disease.

Most diseases are due to a disruption of our microbiome, and the common causes of this disruption is deficiency and toxicity. Essentially it is either not enough vitamins and minerals, too much of something, like mercury or parasites, a compromised system of digestion, or all three.

So how do we tend to our aquariums better, and keep the ecosystem balanced supporting not only our mouth, but the rest of our body? According to the World Health Organization, 2.4 billion people suffer from untreated tooth decay in their permanent teeth, with 621 million children facing untreated decay in their baby teeth. That's one third of the world's population suffering from untreated cavities, and it's preventable!

According to the American Dental Association, periodontal disease is "a chronic infection that can result in the destruction of tooth supporting structures (i.e., the gingiva, periodontal ligament, and alveolar bone) and eventual tooth loss." Forty-seven percent of adults over thirty, and seventy percent of adults over sixty-five have periodontal disease. We can see that this is a widespread and common phenomenon. If our biome is balanced, we can prevent cavities and periodontitis along with all the other issues that stem from these two imbalances. Including toxic amalgams, silent tooth infections, missing teeth, root canals, absorbing bacteria and toxins into our blood stream, and triggering inflammation leading to all the systemic diseases we've already discussed.

So where do we begin?

Let's start with our saliva. There are two types, mucus and serous, as well as two types of bacteria in our mouths, aerobic and anaerobic. For the best biome conditions, we should strive for a balance.

Ever wonder how some people don't really brush and floss but hardly ever get cavities? And why is it that others are so diligent about their oral hygiene, yet it seems like every time they go to the dentist, they have yet another cavity? "I have soft teeth" they say. Or maybe, it's the health and quality of their saliva?

Ever wonder why cats and dogs never get cavities?

These animals generally eat a diet lower in carbohydrates, with a higher salivary pH, and larger gaps between teeth. Making flossing unnecessary for man's best friends. They also take every opportunity to chew on hard materials like bones and sticks, slippers, and recently purchased furniture, which makes them mostly impervious to those oral problems we humans need to contend with.

As a result, cavity-producing bacteria do not thrive in their mouths. The effective result is a cavity-free guarantee. They are, however, prone to periodontitis. So why is that?

Cats and dogs eat a diet primarily composed of meat. Instead of feeding aerobic acid producing bacteria, like sugar and carbohydrates do, it feeds anaerobic bacteria that tend to inflame and damage the gums.

You can have cavities, or you can have periodontal disease, but you can't have both!

You either over feed the aerobic bacteria or the anaerobic bacteria. If you overfeed the aerobic bacteria with sugars, they make acid and you get enamel erosion and cavities. If you overfeed the pathogenic anaerobic bacteria with meat or kill off the aerobic with toxins and allow the pathogenic anaerobic bacteria to overgrow you get a gum infection.

But if you have both bacteria in balance... you get neither!

HEAL 'EM DON'T DRILL 'EM

So now you know that we can prevent cavities by balancing our biome, decreasing the acid producing bacteria, and increasing the pH of our saliva. Let's talk about reversing, and healing the cavities we already have by remineralizing the enamel, instead of drilling and filling those beautiful, perfectly sculpted molars.

Biomimetic (mimicking nature) dentistry improves on traditional dentistry in that it embraces the goal of restoration through conservative treatment options. These options "mimic" the properties of natural teeth and strive to preserve pulp vitality which restores structural integrity to the oral cavity. Biomimetic dentistry minimizes excessive preparation for crowns and reduces the need for root canals. It gives hope for badly damaged teeth that may be deemed "un-restorable".

When we combine several techniques from traditional, five-thousand-year-old Chinese medicine, and the technologically advanced Western medicine, using biology, technology, and psychology, we create a favorable healing environment for patients.

Think of it as a three-step life-changing protocol.

Transilluminators are fiber optic instruments that produce a high intensity white light that is focused via a thin probe which is used to detect tiny, insipient cavities. This is a wonderful adjunct technique to see if we need to do a filling or if we can remineralize a weak area of the tooth. Diagnostic lasers can help detect hidden cavities on pits and fissures of teeth. If there are weak areas, we use a paste that increases the pH back to alkaline levels, and provides the body with the necessary minerals topically, and systemically to remineralize the enamel.

Calcium sulfate and CCP (casein calcium-binding peptides) literally reinforces the enamel making the tooth harder and less soluble to acid. If you catch the erosion early, and are diligent, you can remineralize the tooth in about two months. However, insurance companies won't pay for simple solutions to complicated problems. They just cover the filling and drilling treatment, so often dentists opt to do that for their patients.

This perverse incentive has significant risks and downsides.

We know that the oral cavity is plush with capillaries and blood supply to absorb nutrients as we discussed earlier. It is just as susceptible to absorbing toxins and bacteria. If you drill down through the enamel and tooth decay, you inevitably create the environment for these bacteria and toxins to be released and absorbed into the body. This increases systemic inflammation and can contribute to atherosclerosis (plaques in your arteries) as well as stoke risk and embolisms. Breathing the drilled plaque introduces bacteria and toxins into your lungs can lead to lung infections.

Instead, spend some time in the sunshine so you can produce some bone building vitamin D, use the remineralization paste ($20), optimize the pH of your saliva, and there's a good chance you can heal those early cavities, and avoid the drama!

Sounds much more pleasant and constructive to me.

So, the best advice I can offer you is, be your own advocate. Do your research. Ask questions. Find out why they are recommending what they are offering you. Does it make sense for you or for them? Find an open-minded, well-rounded practitioner to help you get the results you want.

If you plan to live to 100 vibrant, productive, and fulfilling years, optimizing the oral cavity and keeping your teeth for a lifetime, is of utmost importance.

～

FINAL THOUGT

"Life in all its fullness is mother nature
obeyed." – Weston A. Price, DDS

Chapter 12

YOUTHFUL LONGEVITY

Living to 100 Vibrant, Productive, and Fulfilling
Years is Your Birthright, and Mandate.

A fisherman ran through the small village, near a stormy ocean, knocking on each door and warning that a great flood is coming. Most people grabbed some things, said their thanks, and ran for their lives. But as he came up to the last home and knocked on the door, all he heard as a reply to his frantic calls to evacuate, was a muffled and confident "no thank you, GD will save me."

As the water crashed onto the streets and began to rise, a boat pulled up to his second-floor window, the driver pleading with the man to get in so they can take him to safety. "No thank you, GD will save me," he answered. Finally, as the man sat on the roof of his house with the water splashing about his shoulders, a helicopter appeared overhead with the rescue crew almost begging the praying man to grab the rope so they can pull him aboard and save his life. "No thank you, GD will save me," he answered, now struggling to keep his head above water.

Well, as I'm sure you already know, the man drowned.

When this good and faithful servant finally appeared before GD. In a somber and petulant voice, he asked: Lord I believed in you, every day I prayed to you, and I spent my life serving you. How could you, in my hour

Ikigai

of need, allow me to perish so tragically? Trying His best to remain calm, and not pierce this fool with a lightning rod, the Lord finally answered in his booming and sonorous voice: who do you think sent the fisherman, the boat, and the helicopter?!!

There is a natural order to the universe, the Daoist explains this timeless idea through the concept of Yin and Yang. Represented in the famous round, black and white symbol, with each color bleeding into the other, and hosting a small round island of the opposite color in each. Not necessarily only the conflicting opposites, as in good and evil, love and hate, or fire and water. But forces that work in unison, and have a unique syngeneic relationship, as in the feminine and the masculine.

They are opposite in some ways. Sure.

But only when working in concert can they become one, and as if through some supernatural sorcery, this unremarkable man and simple woman, can come together and literally manifest GD-like power and create life. The unique, complex, and beautiful kind. Potentially replicating themselves many times over and becoming so much more than what the individual self is capable of on its own.

In some ways, life and death as well complement each other, albeit in a way less clear to the naked eye of the average person, and far outside the limits of our understanding. We have no idea where we came from and had little to say about the prospect of being born. Millions of serendipitous events had to come together going back generations, perhaps all the way to Adam and Eve, before this miracle that you are, had a chance to manifest. One day we just appear, and by the time we are aware of our presence and purpose, we've been here for decades. Similarly, we have very little to say about the when and how of dying, and don't really know what happens after we're done doing that. We just have to leave it up to the same Creator who brought us here, and trust that once we complete this journey, that there is something at least as miraculous and beautiful on the other side of that mysterious transition as we got to experience for the briefest of moments on this green earth.

Perhaps so much more so.

Someday I will die, and if current statistics are a guide, then it will most probably be from either cancer, heart disease, or iatrogenic injury. And, it may very well be after my hundredth birthday, or perhaps after this afternoon tea. In the grand scheme of things, there is not much I can do about that somewhat gloomy inevitability, and in a hundred years no one will care. But if I refuse to listen to the clear and obvious warnings being sent to me one after the other, then the only person I can blame for my lugubrious health, lamentable suffering, and untimely demise, is me.

Does it really matter if I live less than eighty years, or beyond a hundred, to anyone but me? Is it worth the effort to try living longer, and if it is then for what purpose? If one is not enjoying life, and if they consider each day a struggle that feels more like torture, why would they want to work to extend it any more than necessary? On the other hand, we will be dead, much longer than we get to be alive in this remarkable world. That's the undeniable thing about eternity, it lasts a very, very long time, and who knows how we're going to like being there, forever.

I mean, I can hardly wait for the light to turn green.

So, if we won the conception lottery, got passed all the hazards of being born, and entered this fairytale world without too much drama. Got taken care of well enough as children so that we are still here as adults, me writing and you reading, then it is a blessing worth celebrating. Somehow a few of us have been chosen to experience this brief moment in time, in this magical world of white clouds, blue oceans, laughing children, breathtaking sunsets, latte-art cappuccinos, and dark chocolate. Would we not want it to last as long as possible.

As long as we were promised.

"My spirit shall not abide in man forever, for he is flesh; his days shall be a hundred and twenty years." - GD, all time bestselling author of the Bible.

Certainly, we all know that living to 120 is impossible, since you and I never met anyone who has been able to live that long. Except that on August fourth of 1997 a simple woman who was living in Aries, France died. It would not be news or of interest to anyone but her family, if not for the documented fact that at the time or her passing she was 122 years and 164 days old, and in good health her entire life. Jean was definitely not health minded or had any interest in longevity, as she smoked cigarettes till she was 117 and drank port wine regularly.

Perhaps the quote "the man who says it can't be done is constantly being interrupted by someone doing it" is exceptionally apropos.

A course that I took some decades ago proposed the idea that life is empty and meaningless, and it does not mean anything that it's empty and meaningless. When I first heard this theory, I of course had issues with this nihilistic proposition, as in my own life I made everything mean everything. A certain look, a particular tone, an action or inaction, rain or shine, could all be interpreted in a way that would either produce anger or sadness, depression or euphoria, fight or flight. But of course, any meaning we give to our existence is just that, our own manufactured perception based on interpretation of events, as well as education, religion, and the tribe to which we belong and are nurtured by.

Ultimately, the only reality is that we are born one day, and that one day we will die. So perhaps it's not "death and taxes" the lighthearted phrase famously coined by Benjamin Franklin, as the only permanency, but conception and conclusion, consciousness and oblivion, day and night. It is a fact that what has a beginning also must have an end, which is the only true certainty in this world. So, thinking of life as this empty slate, a blank canvas if you will, allows for a tremendous amount of freedom, serenity, and power to establish the kind of belief systems that generate actions which are the true expression of who we are at the deepest levels of what it means to be a unique human being. The driving force propelling and guiding us in the direction of our true purpose. That incomprehensible and nebulous something that compelled Shakespeare to write "that this above all, *to thine own self be true, and then it must follow as the night the day, thou canst not then be false to any man."*

THE ROOT OF AGING

After selling his company to Pay Pal for $800 million dollars in 2013, Bryan Johnson, the forty-six-year-old entrepreneur and biohacker, has set his sights on youthful longevity as the next frontier. Spending some two million dollars per year on diagnostic testing and consultation with top optimization doctors and scientists in the world. He is on the forefront of breaking that four-minute mile of human potential to live as long and as well as possible. Bryan is a little bit extreme to say the least, with a very strict diet, "where each calorie has to fight for its life" a sleep regimen that has him in bed by 8:30 pm, and the consumption of 111 supplements every day. He famously had a plasma transfusion from his seventeen-year-old son, to stave off the aging process, so he can look and feel younger.

He also allegedly injects Botox into the little johnson for better sexual performance.

I'm sure you, like me, have some feelings about that kind of thing. But in the beginning of the twentieth century, it was wealthy and eccentric people like him who invested a fortune in the purchase of the horseless carriage. Very impractical at the time, as there were just a few that were made available, all built by hand, and out of reach for everyone but the super-rich. In fact, after the Benz Motorwagen was patented on July 3, 1886, within the next ten years, only 25 were built. There were no roads, highways, gas stations, or infrastructure of any kind. And I'm sure this primitive contraption got some strange looks from people used to seeing the only kind of carriages humanity has ever known for most of its existence, till that moment in time. But just a little over a century later, when we hear someone does not own a car or does not know how to drive one, we think it somewhat strange. Today cars are ubiquitous around the world and are such an ingrained part of our reality that we could not imagine life without them.

A study recently published in the journal of Nature Aging, explores the decade long work of Keiko Kono, assistant professor of membranology of Japan's Okinawa Institute of Science and Technology, on the future in which people essentially function at the peak level of health expression right up until the moment they die, and hopefully sometime after their hundredth birthday. Senescence, in the human body, happens when the cell goes to the limits of its replication capabilities and loses the power of division, buoyancy, and growth. Spinning out of control like a punctured helium balloon, it begins to wreak havoc on other cells and systems of the body. Each cell has a fragile membrane that is many times thinner than a soap bubble and is susceptible to damage from oxidative stress. Kind of like when you cut an apple in half and leave it out on the table for a long time. Although the body has the innate capacity to repair those assaults, as we get older this process becomes more frantic, labored, and less effective. We then lose flexibility, recovery, and function, and start developing age related conditions and diseases.

Now that science has zeroed in on the underlying cause of what is actually at the root of the aging process, we can imagine that the world's brightest minds can focus on figuring out how to slow it down and perhaps, in the near future, help us reach for the very pinnacle of youthful longevity unhampered. It may be through a combination of nutrition, supplements, fitness, lifestyle, genetics, lasers, AI, and medications, but all signs are showing that humanity is about to embark on an entirely new frontier and test its limitations.

THE LONGEVITY LAW

If you take a moment to think about it, the way we structured all the knowledge about the human body, and the systems of health care delivery, is somewhat strange. It's like having access to the kind of computer power able to solve poverty entirely but using it exclusively to manage the distribution of food stamps, managing soup kitchens, and printing welfare checks. After banking, which is the largest industry in the United States, the next three are pharmaceuticals, hospitals, and medical insurance, respectively. With all that wealth, power, and brilliance focused on either managing well established symptoms, emergency room visits, or end of life care.

There is also this bizarre relationship between your employer and "health" insurance, where it's expected to be part of the compensation package. If you leave the job or are fired, technically you lose that safety net until you find a new place to work. But what does your employer have to do with your health, and why are these two seemingly unrelated parts of life, so inexplicably intertwined? It's about as logical as tying your gym membership to your groceries. Paying a monthly fee high enough to include eggs, butter, and cheese that you can pick up for free at your local supermarket. Of course, after you meet your high deductible, and small co-pay.

It's a little strange, wouldn't you say?

In his paradigm shifting book *'Lifespan: Why We Age and Why We Don't Have To'*, David Sinclair, PhD who spent thirty years at Harvard University studying human longevity in his laboratory, explains the science behind our biological and genetic design, seemingly engineered for a much healthier and longer life. In it he says, *"there is no biological law that says we must age"* and quotes the Nobel Prize-winning physicist Richard Feynman who said: *"There is nothing in biology yet found that indicates the inevitability of death. This suggests to me that it is not at all inevitable and that it is only a matter of time before biologists discover what it is that is causing us the trouble."*

In the following 400 or so neuron-stimulating pages of his book, Dr. Sinclair shares fascinating science, experiments, philosophy, and technology that has me convinced that we can be healthier longer, avoid many modern lifestyle diseases, get to the root of chronic illness before it turns into a health catastrophe, while attaining ageless beauty, and youthful longevity. And as futuristic as it sounds, even identify and edit troublesome genetics using CASPR-cas9, a gene editing technology that earned Microbiologist Emanuelle Charpentier, and Biochemist Jennifer Doudna the Nobel Prize in 2020, and has already been used to successfully treat Sickle Cell Disease in humans. This molecular scissor, as it's called, is able to cut out the cause of potentially devastating disease, at the very taproot.

After reading and digesting this empowering book, his assertion that aging is going to be significantly easier to treat than well-established diseases like cancer, is a paradigm shift worthy of optimistic consideration.

But perhaps more impressively, he explains why up until this moment in time, the entire focus of all the great minds and treasure has been on the management of disparate and innumerable symptoms of well-established disease states. Turns out that up until recently the only classification that could go on a death certificate is the condition that caused it. So, you could die from cancer, heart disease, liver sclerosis, Alzheimer's, diabetes or kidney disease, but the one thing you could not die from was 'old age' itself, because it was never categorized as a cause of death.

All of that changed, when on June 18, 2018, the World Health Organization (WHO) came out with the International Classification of Disease known as ICD11, which may not mean much to you and me but in the scientific circles they may as well have signed the Declaration of Independence from the ravages of age-related symptomatology, and untimely death. Thus, setting forth an entirely new relationship in what is possible for humanity moving forward, to live longer and healthier lives. Because in it, someone added the MG2A Old Age Classification, which designates aging as a disease. And if it is a disease, it can be treated, and resources made available towards testing the limits of our potential for optimal life-long function and youthful longevity.

As encouraging as this is, one can't help but wonder, why was this self-evident and practical idea not always the case? And, if you permit me this quick aside, what is an alien group like the World Health Organization, currently run by the Ethiopian born Tedros Adhanoum Ghebreysus, PhD who was a member of the Marxist, Tigray Peoples Liberation Front (TPLF), with a suspicious allegiance to China's Communist Party, and who himself is not a medical doctor, doing telling the citizens of this nation what to do and how to interact with their system of health care?

At what point and under whose authority did we vote to surrender our sovereignty to a foreign body of unaccountable bureaucrats, as capable and well-meaning as they may be?

Forgive me, but them is some third-world shenanigans worthy of investigation.

According to the National Cancer Institute, the US government allocated 7.22 billion dollars towards cancer research for the fiscal year 2024. Since cancer is recognized as a disease, public funds are made available to finance the ongoing fifty-year war against it, declared on December 23, 1971, by President Richard Nixon. The same President Richard Nixon who oversaw the devastating defeat of another famous war that still haunts our national consciousness.

Since then, some 90 billion dollars have been spent researching what has been historically and for the most part, a disease of aging. Of course, I realize that for some reason, be that environment, chemicals, pollution or nutrition, this scourge has grown more viscous and ubiquitous, affecting all age groups indiscriminately. Usually, however, it's people who are fifty and older who have a much higher risk of developing cancer, and over thirty percent of those who are seventy-five and beyond will be diagnosed with this callous disease. Until recently little to nothing was available to try and understand 'aging' as the root cause most responsible for many of the potentially terminal conditions, like cancer.

For fiscal 2023, some 3.9 billion dollars were allocated by congress for the National Institute on Aging (NIA) up from 3.5 billion in 2018, but as Dr. Sinclair laments in his book, most of that budget is used to research the prognosis of disease and disability and to study the lives of seniors. Unfortunately, however, less than three percent of the funding for "aging research" was allocated to study the biology of aging itself that could perhaps ameliorate the cause of many age-related diseases. Despite that, a tremendous number of breakthroughs and interest has been stirred up in this area. Known as geoscience, many of the leaders in functional medicine are speaking and writing books on the topic of living longer, healthier, and more productive lives, that are becoming fast bestsellers.

TRUTH SHALL SET US FREE

Practically speaking, by 2040 there will be some 81 million people in the United States over sixty-five, that's almost 30% of the population. The old Great Society paradigms will no longer apply as this idea of idle retirement and having generous access to free medical care and social security for decades on end will go the way of the pet rock. According to the US Department of Housing and Urban Development, there were 653,104 homeless adults in the nation in 2023, with 38.3% of that number women, as well as a mind numbing, 2.5 million children.

If that is not evidence of the fraying of this safety net, I'm not sure what is.

When signed into law, the Social Security Act of 1935 had a few things going for it. First the worker-to-beneficiary ratio was 150 to 1, which means that for every person receiving benefits there were 150 working and contributing to the system. Second, the average white male at that time lived to 61 years of age, while the average white female to 65 (for black Americans it was 51.3 and 55.2 respectively). Basically, with the retirement age set at 66, the idea was that most people would be dead by the time they were eligible to collect what they ostensibly paid in for their 'rocking-chair' benefits.

Over the last hundred years many realities have changed in our society, but we continued to pass along what was a temporary fix to a complicated, long-term problem from one generation to the next like a decomposing paper cup. So today, we're living much longer, there are fewer people in the workplace, medicine has evolved to provide some very complex and expensive procedures, and the birthrate has dropped precipitously over the last hundred years. Of course that was before the mRNA experiments forced on our unwitting young people, dropping the birthrate another 13-20% according to the research done by Dr. Naomi Wolf, in her fantastic book *"Facing the Beast: Courage Faith and Resistance in a New Dark Age"*.

It is estimated that by 2040, for every person receiving Social Security benefits, two will be working, as opposed to the already exhausted and frustrated three, today.

Honestly, growing up I never liked mathematics, but I was never this terrified of them either.

Maybe one day some brave politician will go up to the Presidential podium, adjust the mic, clear his throat and say something to the effect of the following:

My fellow Americans, this great nation was founded on the principles of free enterprise, hard work, ingenuity, frugality, and independence. But somewhere along the way we began embracing those failed collectivist ideas that our founding fathers abhorred, and that our brave soldiers fought against on battlefields around the world.

Today I must tell you that Social Security and Medicare are the largest Ponzi schemes ever perpetrated on humanity. They have at this moment run their course and will henceforth be repealed. We can no longer afford to print money with abandon, and if we tax our citizens any further, they will have no choice but to revolt. That is why as of today I am implementing the Small Government act of 2028. Our total budget will be shrunk to just 15% of the GDP and we will no longer be involved in the fiscal, personal, or health concerns of our constituents.

We understand that as public servants our primary purpose, according to the Tenth Amendment of the US Bill of Rights, is to defend this great nation from enemies foreign and domestic. Be the neutral and unbiased referee in the market. Protect intellectual and private property. Maintain the infrastructure of our bridges, tunnels, and roads, and keep our cities safe through smart policing. All else we will leave up to you, the Citizen of these United States. As this is a nation of the people, for the people, and by the people.

Thank you, good night, and GD Bless America!!

TAKE ME TO YOUR LEADERS

The undisputed pioneer of this longevity revolution is Mark Hyman, MD who recently came out with his latest book, *"Young Forever: With a Step-by-step Programme to Reverse Disease, Ease Pain, and Renew Energy"*. In addition to that, he is a fifteen-time NYT bestselling author, practicing physician, and senior advisor for the Cleaveland Clinic Center for Functional Medicine.

Some fifteen years ago, after I introduced him to about 500 people crammed into the ballroom of our conference and he completed his visionary, hope filled, and somewhat iconoclastic ScHO Keynote presentation. Mark pulled out a case of his newly released, the *"UltraSimple Diet: Kick-Start Your Metabolism and Safely lose up to 10 Pounds in 7 Days"* and invited those who would like a copy to peacefully and patriotically come up to the front of the stage, and inadvertently almost started a riot. It was a scene out of a rock concert gone wild, as people scrambled and fought to get their hands on the few available copies.

It was then I realized, and contrary to popular belief, that intelligent people care about their health.

Very much so.

In addition to some of the books I already mentioned, Cameron Diaz has written one called, the *"Longevity Book: The Science of Aging, The Biology of Strength, and the Privilege of Time"* published in 2016. It is a fascinating look at this topic from the perspective of someone who depended on her looks as an actress, but is exploring aging from the inside out, scientific, philosophical, and holistic perspective. On the very first page there is a remarkable photo of Cameron, taken when she was just sixteen years old, held by her when she was twenty-two, and then when she was twenty-eight, and finally at forty-four.

When she first entered the business of modeling and acting, her photographer suggested that after this first photo shoot, they should repeat it every six or so years. If anything is the physical manifestation of ageless beauty, this unique, multi-dimensional, time-lapse photograph is it. Cameron is aging on purpose and over her adult lifetime has been a student of nutrition, exercise, and the cultivation of longevity habits, as she keeps an eye on the latest scientific developments and breakthroughs.

I'll bet you a nickel she'll live to be at least a hundred.

Then there's Sergey Young, considered the "Top-100 Longevity Leader" author of "*The Science and Technology of Growing Young: An Insider's Guide to the Breakthroughs that will Dramatically Extend Lifespan ... and What You Can Do Right Now*" and development sponsor of the Age Reversal XPRIZE, with a hundred-and-one-million-dollar purse awarded to those who can successfully turn back the clock and expand human lifespan. In this brilliant book, Sergey is inviting us to consider that "living to 200 years of age is no longer science fiction."

Published in May of 2021 *"Radical Longevity: The Powerful Plan to Sharpen Your Brain, Strengthen Your Body, and Reverse the Symptoms of Aging"*, by Ann Louis Gittleman, PhD who is a bestselling and award-winning author with thirty-five books to her credit, explores the science behind nutrition, specifically aimed at providing the body with everything it needs to live longer and be healthier, using a knife and fork as the main tools. It includes a recipe for the "Live Longer Cocktail" with cranberry juice, cinnamon, and chia seeds, of course.

The legendary cardiologist turned wellness evangelist, the iconic Steven R. Gundry, MD who was the keynote speaker at our very last ScHO conference in NYC, held near Times Square in November 2019. Right before fluemageddon turned the world upside down. Recently he came out with *"The Longevity Paradox: How to Die Young at a Ripe Old Age."* In this wonderful book he introduces us to Akkermancia an important bug found in abundance of the digestive microbiome of those people living over a 100, as they sit in small coffee shops, passionately discussing world affairs, belly laughing, and enjoying youthful longevity.

When Mitchell Kurk, MD, DO, OD wrote the timeless *"Prescription for Long Life: Essential Remedies for Longevity"* some twenty years ago, he was a youthful, spry, and red-cheeked seventy-three-year-old. Today he is as sharp as he was then, with a great sense of humor, a curious mind, and a busy schedule. I am in his office regularly as he is not only someone I've known for decades and consider a friend, but he is also one of the great minds who consults our team of ScHO Practitioners.

After receiving his doctorate in 1960, Dr. Kurk was practicing the standard allopathic medicine that he was taught at the Philadelphia College of Osteopathic Medicine. It was his wife's diagnosis with a brain tumor in the early 1970's that sent him to longevity and wellness centers around the world, in search of the most innovative approaches to resolve the underlying cause of her terminal illness. Sadly, by the time he started to get some insight into these ancient and futuristic options, his wife already had surgery and chemotherapy. Not long after, the treating physician said that there was nothing else they could do for her, and that "you should get her affairs in order."

Although using all the things he was learning Dr. Kurk was only able to perhaps extend her life and its quality, by just a couple of years. He became a life-long student of 'holistic' medicine and used it for the next five decades to help countless people resolve the underlying cause of their chronic illnesses and achieve youthful longevity. I met and spoke with many of his patients as they sat in the waiting room of his retro office. Ladies in their nineties, who are thin and healthy, and move, look, and sound many decades younger.

When I ask Dr. Kurk why he did not retire at 67 like everyone else, he laughs, "what am I going to do play golf, I don't play golf!" He loves his work, is helping lots of people, keeps himself busy and needed, and at an impressive and vibrant ninety-three, he is an inspiration and the embodiment of his youthful longevity philosophy. As many of my own friends are entering their sixth decade, they are all talking about retirement and the symptoms of aging. I can see this contagious mindset and how it's affecting their behavior, outlook, and level of activity.

In my mind you retire once you are terminally sick, unable to think, or have a job you hate. But if you are living your mission, sharing your hard-earned wisdom, and building a great cathedral that will serve humanity for generations, why would you ever want to stop doing that unless you are forced.

Permanently parking your earthly vessel at some lonely pier as you get dull, and fat, and old.

You know how sometimes when you plan to go out for dinner on the weekend, and you're like 'what do you want to eat?' And she's like 'I don't know, what do you want to eat?' Now imagine that every single day and at infinitum. I can see why people who retire early don't live long after they do.

They don't want to.

When juxtaposed with someone like my friend Dr. Kurk, it's clear that "old" is psychology not chronology.

For his fifty-nineth birthday, Jeffrey Life, MD, PhD received a framed photograph from his ex-wife as a gift. It was of him sitting shirtless on the back of a boat from a couple of years back. This was not a flattering picture. As he looked like virtually every other American man of that age. About fifty pounds heavier than a healthy BMI, big belly, dark circles, deep wrinkles, and what can only be called breasts. He was lethargic, had an atrophying muscular frame, with full blown type 2 diabetes, out of control blood sugar, and an undiagnosed heart condition.

He looked and felt old.

Today, at eighty-six, Dr. Life is coming out with his fourth book *"The Longevity Life Plan: The Pathway to Living Beyond 100 with Strength, Vitality, Purpose and Grit!"* He is perhaps the perfect man to talk about achieving youthful longevity because just a few years after he saw that photo of himself on that boat, he was chosen by Men's Fitness Magazine as one of the top twenty-five fittest men of the year. If you see Dr. Life on the cover of one of his books, it looks like his head was photoshopped onto the frame of a thirty-year-old body builder.

It wasn't.

In 2011, after coming out with his NYT bestselling book *"The Life Plan: How any Man Can Achieve Lasting Health, Great Sex, and Stronger, Leaner Body"* we invited Dr. Life to speak at a few of our conferences, both in NYC and on Long Island, where he delivered his message to full ballrooms of standing room only crowds of both men, and women. I learned a tremendous amount from Dr. Life as far as nutrition, fitness, and hormones, but more importantly, I've been inspired by the possibility of proactive aging on an entirely different level.

He too has no plans to retire.

The last book I will mention here is *"100 IS THE NEW 30: How Playing the Symphony of Longevity will Enable Us to Live Young for a Lifetime"* by Jeffrey Gladden, MD, published in August of 2023. When I first heard the title, I was a little put off as it seemed a bit over the top. But as I read its almost 500 pages, I got a better insight into what the author was trying to say. As an avid surfer, mountain biker, and snowboarder, he does not behave his age, because we're not really sure what his age is. In our recent interview Dr. Gladden shared that although he recently celebrated his seventieth chronological birthday, most of the physical and biological markers that matter are that of a 30-year-old, or younger. This is not your "eat more broccoli, exercise, and avoid sugar" kind of book. As it delves deep into the latest science and technology for human optimization and youthful longevity at a level I've never seen before.

After having experienced the natural aging process of our overstressed, toxic, and undernourished society, he was overweight, lethargic, and depressed. By his fifty's he looked like one those new 'modern man' mannequins with a pot belly, a blank stare, and no energy or desire to move. His personal transformation and ability to crack the code of youthful longevity allows Dr. Gladden to enjoy life at an entirely different pace. While looking his best and fittest self as he is doing it. This is a miracle born of proactive science and lifestyle modification worth acknowledging.

Dr. Gladden, as well, considers retirement anathema.

He has a detailed plan of what he wants to achieve before his 100th birthday, as he aims to stretch human potential to live a longer and healthier life, for himself and his many clients.

By no means is this an exhaustive list of great people or books on the topic of youthful longevity, but as I lay out my case, I want to present all the credible evidence showing beyond the benefit of a doubt, that our system of health care is about to go through a major transformation.

Today, it is accepted that we must develop a symptom before our 'health' insurance, one that we're paying a large and growing portion of our income for, will reluctantly approve some band aids and aspirin to treat it. At the same time, we don't give much thought to the quality of the food and drink we consume, and whether it has the nutrition necessary to power us effectively and efficiently for the duration of our productive and fulfilling lives. We have no idea of our vitamin and mineral levels and have no way to track the efficacy of our digestive biome. We don't know if our environment is introducing heavy metals, parasites, or mold to our bodies on a daily basis, and we don't know if our genetics are able to detoxify them efficiently.

This bizarre moment in the history of mankind will be known as the "Stoned Ages." As no one in the future will understand how those brilliant people, who built one of the most remarkable societies in the history of human existence, could be so misled, abused, and robbed of their most valuable possession.

Time.

My dear friend, please give me the gift of your undivided attention for just a moment longer, as I propose and affirm that living till 100 vibrant, productive, and fulfilling years is your birthright, and mandate. It is written in the book of life and promised by the Creator of all that is right and pure and good. While the forces of evil that profit from your sickness, disease, and helplessness, are gathering like dark, ominous clouds, twisting, and howling for more.

On behalf, and at the behest of all the passionate, honorable, and courageous doctors and healers mentioned, and the many who were not, I will continue knocking on your proverbial door till my hand bleeds.

Because a great flood is coming.

$\sim$

FINAL THOUGHT

"I've learned that the secret to longevity is enjoying every minute of your life." – Jean Louise Calment

EPOLOGUE

If you could imagine some sinister character, the likes of Mister Evil perhaps, who is sitting in an elaborate bunker petting his ugly Canadian Sphynx and thinking diabolical thoughts, about how to steal the most valuable commodity on this planet.

You would not be far off.

There is just no way that we got to this nefarious place organically. All the good people getting up each day and working hard providing products and services to improve the lives of their fellow man. Driven by the invisible hand, the laws of the land, and the 'do on to others' dictate. Then, within just a few decades we have an unsustainable system of healthcare, reaching five trillion dollars per year, and a population of our fellow citizens who are some of the sickest, pharmaceutically dependent, and most obese people in the history of mankind.

It is obvious that our health has been abducted.

Mine, in fact, was held hostage for some twenty years, in a dark, cold, and lonely dungeon. And I can tell you unequivocally, without it, there was nothing else. All the things that I imagined I wanted as an ambitious young man, in a nation with all the beautiful, shiny, and luxury things that would bring joy, pride, and security to the people I love, became dull and gray and banal.

We are in a biblical fight of good against evil, and just as in other historic battles the outcome is far from certain. As the cacophony of this struggle is sure to echo through eternity. We're not even sure who it is we are fighting and what it is that we are up against. The only thing we can ascertain is that unless we get wise to their evil plan, and identify the black-hearted ringleaders, the damage will be so severe, the subjugation so complete that there will be no way out.

No way back.

The great thing about our fellow citizens, as far as I can tell as both an outsider and insider, is that once they are inspired, or infuriated, things can change very quickly. It was in 1903 that the Ford Motor Company was founded, and an entire century later in 2003, almost to the day, Tesla finally drove on to the scene. In all that time just three companies controlled the entire car market in the United States, and only when this electric vehicle concept with a unique purpose made its debut, the entire industry was upended in a relatively short time. On the other hand, when Anheuser Busch, the iconic American Brewing Company founded in 1876, aligned itself with a message that left consumers who historically bought its light beer option with a bad taste. It took a tremendous hit.

One from which it may never recover.

Over the decades, we've watched our parents, our children, our siblings, and our friends get mercilessly crushed between the six trillion dollar processed food industry and the almost five trillion-dollar disease management industry.

But we stayed silent.

More recently we were subjugated and molested by those mendacious officials and their tyrannical lockdowns, forced medical experimentation, and the resulting mass casualties in the form of 1,273,971 excess deaths in the United States since 2020.

220

And we turned the other cheek.

We watch the 'health' insurance expense grow by double digits from one year to the next, as the access, value, and quality of life-saving care plumets precipitously.

Finally, we clenched our fists.

For decades we permitted a system of care that does not offer the permanent resolution for an early-stage diagnosis, but only seeks to profit from the management of well-established chronic disease for the duration of our life. Allowing what was an easily extinguishable spark to fester and explode into a health catastrophe with inevitable and tragic collateral damage.

And physicians, historically in step with medical dogma, start breaking ranks.

We've seen the health problems of the aged: diabetes, heart disease, and cancer. Trickle down to the youngest and most vulnerable groups like toddlers and kindergarteners.

And the mothers got furious and found their voice.

Regular people, who would otherwise have no interest in our system of 'health' care, but because they were misled, and tormented, and tortured by it, suddenly become passionate advocates. Writing books, speaking publicly, building alliances, and bravely challenging the status quo.

Not since a few rebels from the Thirteen American Colonies who rejected the imperial rule of those they were born under, and ultimately subjugated by, did a revolt to save the body and soul of our nation was so prime for awakening.

Here, we the American people, mothers, fathers, doctors, and patriots of all flavors are finding each other as the winds of change fill our sails, propelling us towards the warm and sunny shores of freedom, prosperity, independence, and youthful longevity.

This will be epic.

Hey, "It's DOCTOR Evil, I didn't spend six years in Evil Medical School to be called "mister," thank you very much." – Dr. Evil

ACKNOWLEDGEMENTS

When I was in the auto repair business, there was virtually no one I could call, who would offer their expert advice and counsel as generously, as so many of the doctors I've met on my travels through this multi-decade healing journey have.

I would like to thank those of you who chose to pursue this noble mission of caring for the health and well-being of your fellow man. And courageous enough to live the purpose that originally grabbed your unwavering interest and earned your tireless effort. I would like to thank all the great doctors who agreed to be a part of our events and interviews and who gave of their time, wisdom, and knowledge about what it takes for us to live longer, healthier, and more prosperous lives.

More specifically, I'd like to thank Danielle Roberts, Joshua Rosenthal, and Jimmy Kilimitzoglou, the remarkable physicians, who encouraged and supported the early stages of this Science of Human Optimization endeavor. Also, I'd like to thank Ilene Castaldo, the Family Nurse Practitioner who was first to join our ScHO program as an expert healer, and all the other FNP's who followed her since.

My gratitude to Clifford Locks, the brilliant businessman and investor, who saw the potential of this message and model, and has been supporting and guiding it from its inception. Your encouragement and advice have been a source of great value.

Our first ScHO clients who were brave enough, and knew me well enough, to join our insipient program and gave life and substance to this tenuous dream. I thank you with the profound gratitude of someone who was blind and whose vision was miraculously restored. And you who took the time to read this book, as well as those who are the future million ScHO clients, we have yet to meet but I already know who you are, and I thank you!

I would like to thank my daughter Bashel, son Adriel, and wife of some 35 years Alina, for their unconditional love, wise counsel, unwavering support, and for being the purpose and driving force that propels me forward.

And most of all I'd like to thank my mamachka Adel, cause she's just awesome.

CO-WRITER BIOGRAPHY

Danielle Roberts, DO [Chapter 9] is a doctor of osteopathy, with a master's in clinical nutrition, she practiced as a Family Practitioner and Hospitalist for a decade. She's earned numerous certifications in Chelation and IV therapies, Reiki, personal training, and group fitness. She is a life-long student of human optimization and youthful longevity.

Joshua Rosenthal, MD [Chapter 10] is a Board-Certified Sleep and Regenerative Medicine Specialist, integrating his expertise in circadian biology, mitochondrial medicine, and photobiomodulation, he helps clients rebuild their mind and body at the cellular and subcellular levels, creating structures for human optimization and youthful longevity.

Dimitrios "Jimmy" Kilimitzoglou, DDS, [Chapter 11] is a renowned Biomimetic Dentist who graduated from Stony Brook University, School of Dental Medicine in 2002. Prior to studying at Dental School, he attended Adelphi University in Garden City, New York where he graduated Magna Cum Laude. With a focus on oral optimization and youthful longevity.

BIOGRAPHY

Alex Lubarsky was born in the USSR, he is the founder of Science of Human Optimization, Inc. a company that brings a more proactive and personalized approach to health care, with a goal of serving a million clients throughout the United States.

Over the last twenty years, he hosted conferences and radio programs that featured speakers like Suzanne Somers, Carol Alt, Mark Hyman, Stephen Gundry, Jack LaLane, and Fran Drescher to name a few. Together with his team of merry men he partnered with major media outlets and brought a hundred thousand guests to the live Youthful Longevity events.

He is the Author of *"The Art of Selling The Art Of Healing: How the Rebels of Today are Creating the Health Care of Tomorrow, and Why Your Life Depends On It."* As well as husband, father, grandfather, and godfather, who lives happily on Long Island, NY, and can't seem to mind his own business or leave well enough alone.

REFERENCES

1. Danielle Roberts, "The Placebo Effect", https://www.drdanielleroberts.com/inquiries/the-placebo-effect
2. Guyer, B. et al., Childhood Mortality Rates by Age at Death; United States 1900-1998, Pediatrics 2000; 106: 1307-1317
3. https://www.cdc.gov/pcd/issues/2024/23_0267.htm
4. Deepak Chopra, "Cancer. A Preventable Disease is Causing a Revolution," Deepak Chopra, August 21st, 2012, https://www.deepakchopra.com/articles/cancer-a-preventable-disease-is-creating-a-revolution/
5. Dr. Brownstein, "The Iodine Doctor: 97% Are Iodine Deficient (How Much You Need)," YouTube, May 15, 2024, https://www.youtube.com/watch?v=1ZLqLbdnEuk
6. Douglas S. Ross, "Thyroid Storm", July 5th 2024, https://www.uptodate.com/contents/thyroid-storm
7. David M Brownstein, MD, "Iodine: Why You Need It. Why you Can't Live Without It" January 1, 2014
8. Karyn Shanks, MD, "Vitamin D: Boost Your Mojo," https://www.karynshanksmd.com/2016/10/14/vitamin-d-boost-your-winter-mojo/
9. Wikipedia, "Folate" https://en.wikipedia.org/wiki/Folate, and "Methylenetetrahydrafolate Reductase," https://en.wikipedia.org/wiki/Methylenetetrahydrofolate_reductase
10. Danielle Roberts, "Gluatione, The Master Antioxidant," 2024 http://www.schoinc.com/
11. Richard Fuller Beng, et al., "Pollution and Health: a Progress Update," Volume 6, Issue 6, e535-e547, June 2022

12. Environmental Working Group, "Body Burden: Pollution in Newborns," July 14, 2005, https://www.ewg.org/research/body-burden-pollution-newborns

13. Datis Kharrazian, "Exposure to Environmental Toxins and Autoimmune Conditions" Integr Med (Encinitas). 2021 Apr; 20(2): 20–24. https://www.ncbi.nlm.nih.gov/pmc/articles/PMC8325494/

Printed in the United States
by Baker & Taylor Publisher Services